Sustainable Urban Supply Chain Management

By Ade Asefeso MCIPS MBA

Copyright 2015 by Ade Asefeso MCIPS MBA
All rights reserved.

First Edition

ISBN-13: 978-1505907339

ISBN-10: 1505907330

Publisher: AA Global Sourcing Ltd
Website: http://www.aaglobalsourcing.com

Table of Contents

Disclaimer 5
Dedication 6
Chapter 1: Introduction 7
Chapter 2: Return on Investment is Driving Supply Chain Sustainability 11
Chapter 3: Trends Driving Greener Supply Chains 19
Chapter 4: Steps to a Greener Supply Chain 23
Chapter 5: Using Optimization to Achieve a Green Supply Chain 29
Chapter 6: Cashing in on Your Green Supply Chain Decisions 33
Chapter 7: How to Make Your Supply Chain More Eco-Conscious 37
Chapter 8: How to Build Sustainability into Your Supply Chain 41
Chapter 9: Application of Supply Chain Sustainability 45
Chapter 10: Developing a Sustainable Supply Chain Strategy 49
Chapter 11: A Comprehensive Strategy 53
Chapter 12: Collaborating for Better Information Management 59
Chapter 13: Share Sustainability Best Practices with Suppliers 61

Chapter 14: Why Sustainable Supply Chains Make Business Sense 63
Chapter 15: Why Companies Top Struggles Lie in Sustainable Supply Chains 69
Chapter 16: The Need to Reduce Your Carbon Footprint 73
Chapter 17: How Businesses Can Save Our Cities 79
Chapter 18: The Crucial Role for Business in Sustainable Economy 83
Chapter 19: A Green Supply Chain Starts in China 85
Chapter 20: Supply Chain Sustainability in Africa 93
Chapter 21: Hong Kong Sustainability Urban Growth 97
Chapter 22: The Rapid Development of Dubai .107
Chapter 23: Sustainable Urban Development in Dubai 113
Chapter 24: Scaling Up Sustainable Urban Growth 117
Chapter 25: Resilient Cities 125
Chapter 26: Sustainability is Everyone's Responsibility 133
Chapter 27: Lessons from the Past and Ideas for the Future 135
Chapter 28: Stakeholders Pressure 145

Disclaimer

This publication is designed to provide competent and reliable information regarding the subject matter covered. However, it is sold with the understanding that the author and publisher are not engaged in rendering professional advice. The authors and publishers specifically disclaim any liability that is incurred from the use or application of contents of this book.

If you purchased this book without a cover you should be aware that this book may have been stolen property and reported as "unsold and destroyed" to the publisher. In this case neither the author nor the publisher has received any payment for this "stripped book."

Dedication

To my family and friends who seems to have been sent here to teach me something about who I am supposed to be. They have nurtured me, challenged me, and even opposed me.... But at every juncture has taught me!

This book is dedicated to my lovely boys, Thomas, Michael and Karl. Teaching them to manage their finance will give them the lives they deserve. They have taught me more about life, presence, and energy management than anything I have done in my life.

Chapter 1: Introduction

There are almost as many definitions of "sustainability" as there are shades of green.

One thing that energy and supply chain experts can agree on, however, is that sustainability is one of the most significant issues facing businesses today.

So how do we define sustainability? How can we create "greener" supply chains? Are there really profit opportunities for companies along the way?

There is no doubt that sustainability is entering a new phase that promises a broad impact on supply chains. It covers the entire organization on the demand side as well as the supply side.

From a supply chain view, you can help the environment and create profit opportunities by taking actions such as:
1. Reducing emissions from manufacturing processes.
2. Utilizing more efficient transportation modes such as LTL (less than truck load) rather than parcel.
3. Ensuring that your distribution network is properly sized for customer needs.
4. Replacing facilities with more modern warehouse technologies that use less energy.

Companies that are ahead of the sustainability curve are the ones writing the rules, cutting costs, avoiding risks, and winning public relations battles. Reducing emissions and energy consumption and realizing greater profits are not mutually exclusive.

Supply chain sustainability is a holistic perspective of supply chain processes and technologies that go beyond the focus of delivery, inventory and traditional views of cost. This emerging philosophy is based on the principle that socially responsible products and practices are not only good for the environment, but are important for long-term profitability.

In practice, supply chain sustainability can include projects to reduce energy cost, any form of waste and application of green technologies within transportation and logistics networks. A larger shift involves a deeper level of collaboration with internal and external supply chain partners to re-examine delivery methods, products, packaging and measurement systems.

Urban supply chain is a hot topic right now, but is it simply a concept that is trending or a realistic new supply chain strategy? Every day in cities across the developed world, multiple trucks and other commercial vehicles enter crowded towns to deliver their goods to businesses, predominately retail outlets and offices, making a number of drop-offs before driving out again. Every day, different trucks and commercial vehicles also enter the city to collect parcels, pallets or other items from the same retail outlets and offices for delivery elsewhere.

In theory, the trucks that deliver goods to city businesses could utilize their capacity to collect and drop off goods for those businesses within their existing distribution run and potentially take further goods, or empty pallets, back to their distribution centre when they have completed their deliveries. UK-based Menzies Distribution, a media logistics provider has set up a separate arm to do just this, building on its recent success of delivering travel brochures after its morning newspapers deliveries have been made. While Wal-Mart in the U.S. announced earlier last year it is brainstorming ideas around asking its customers to deliver purchases made by online buyers.

It could be a win-win situation, with near full utilization for logistics service providers (LSPs), lower costs all round and fewer vehicles on the roads, leading to less congestion and lower emissions.

Yet urban supply chain is unlikely to become a reality in meaningful volumes without incentives in the form of co-operation. One example would be to create true green lanes, where trucks are micro-chipped and given priority at traffic lights, speeding its passage. Another option would be collect all the inbound goods at a distribution centre just outside of town and then use trains or boats or electrical cars to deliver the goods into town, consolidated so there is only one delivery to each address. Of course this is in direct contrast to measures already implemented in urban areas globally restricting access for commercial vehicles during peak times, or tolls/other financial charges.

The limitation here is the willingness to co-operate, both within the industry and from local governments. Competitors will need to share the same space in the DC outside town and the same truck going into town. Some relatively neutral party will be needed to establish the DC outside of town and do the last mile, as well as a collaborative booking mechanism. The issue becomes even more clouded when customer to customer logistics deliveries enter the equation, particularly around privacy, remuneration and accountability.

Clearly there are competitive concerns for LSPs here, who will be worried in equal measure about losing business or margin, or missing out on gaining business through co-operating in a more sustainable urban logistics model. Yet the prevalence of the current Omni-channel model could not have been for-seen a decade ago, so it is in the interests of all involved in the supply chain to remain open to innovation as well as collaboration, particularly where sustainability is enhanced.

This 'blue-sky' thinking may well become a reality in the future, and only seeks to highlight the importance of supply chain businesses sharing data and collaborating with their trading partners to gain greater, and ultimately complete, visibility.

Chapter 2: Return on Investment is Driving Supply Chain Sustainability

Return on investment (ROI) is the second-highest driver of supply chain sustainability initiatives among shippers, third party logistics companies and supply chain solution providers, according to the recent survey we carried out before writing this book.

We surveyed more than 600 professionals, almost 80 percent of the respondents said that ROI was an important driver of sustainability initiatives. Improving customer relations was seen as a slightly more significant driver, while increasing supply chain efficiency was seen as slightly less significant.

Shippers reported the greatest levels of ROI from improving energy efficiency and recycling materials. Around three quarters of respondents reported either very or fairly successful ROI, compared with only 3 percent not seeing benefits from these initiatives.

Other notable responses included strategic warehouse/distribution centre placement, reducing packaging, emission measuring/ reductions, and using more efficient transport modes, all of which saw around 50 percent of shippers reporting either very or fairly successful ROI.

Respondents representing third party logistics companies also reported the greatest levels of ROI from improving energy efficiency, with reducing miles through vehicle re-routing as the next most successful initiative. Again, around three quarters of respondents reported either very or fairly successful ROI, compared with only 3 percent not seeing benefits from these initiatives. Other notable responses included horizontal collaboration with other companies, near and/or green/environmental sourcing, emission measuring/reductions, and using more efficient road vehicles, all of which saw around 50 percent of shippers reporting either very or fairly successful ROI.

The Environmental Defence Fund recently released "The Good Haul," a report detailing ten ways to reduce the environmental impact of the shipping sector. Trucking companies, meanwhile, will be under increasing pressure to adopt "green" initiatives as food producers and retailers seek sustainable supply chains, while European industry groups are urging policy makers to establish a voluntary public-private sustainable freight transport partnership.

How can communities, cities and regions support the transition towards sustainable futures?

Cities and regional centres are the engines of economic and cultural growth. High percentage of world population live in them, contributing over 80 per cent of GDP and associated economic and employment growth however, this era of urban-based prosperity is being challenged by the side-effects of success, including regional disparities resulting from unequal and uneven development, the rising ecological footprints of cities, social unease, road congestion, resource scarcity and escalating living costs.

With an emphasis on the values of sustainability, resilience appropriate development and social inclusion, We shall look at the following 13 themes.

1. Urban policy and planning

Studies of urban policy and planning should include a focus on questions of urban governance and political economy, development regulation, metropolitan strategic planning, peri-urban development, the need for and conflicts around urban consolidation and urban renewal, urban infrastructure and transport and urban mobility systems.

2. Place and health

In response to the increasing importance of creating 'healthy places' in the planning and design of new residential communities and revitalizing established ones, this theme investigates the production, experience and governance of health and wellbeing in urban environments in the context of climate change adaptation, sustainability and social inclusion.

3. Environmental management

This theme examines the diverse drivers of ecosystem change, particularly in urban and semi-rural environments. Its aim is to address the gap between conservation theory and real world practice in complex planning environments. Research includes studies of biodiversity planning, natural resource planning, water security and pollution control.

4. Housing studies

Research in this theme focuses on the areas of housing economics, housing policy, homelessness, housing and particular demographic groups (such as immigrants, the aged, etc.) and housing within the urban planning framework. Housing affordability is a critical focus for research as 'housing wealth' is a major determinant of social and economic wellbeing and governments are reducing the provision of public housing to only the most needy.

5. Sustainable built environments

This theme develops strategies and tools for sustainable construction management and procurement, environmental performance assessment and modelling of buildings, innovative building materials and fabrication, retrofitting for climate change, and building life-cycle assessment.

6. Urban metabolism and low-carbon systems

Research towards advancing sustainable production and consumption systems includes; closed loop design, product stewardship, life-cycle assessment, eco-foot-printing, environmental assessment and modelling.

7. Smart cities

This theme recognises the growing importance of collaborative informal learning and its contribution both to promoting balanced economic, social and environmental development in city-regions, and addressing urban challenges. New information and communication technologies are a particularly important resource in some smart city initiatives.

8. Resilient regions

Cities are reliant upon the regions that supply the resources necessary for human health, social wellbeing and economic productivity; however pressures from globalization, national development strategies and global environmental climate change are undermining the capacity of regions to contribute to supply the needs of cities. At the same time, other resource rich regions are experiencing "boom" conditions and the impacts of overly –fast, reactive development. Policies and strategies that support sustainable regional development and build resilience to the impacts of change are the focus of this research theme.

9. Urban education

Social learning is central to sustainable cities and regions. Research focuses on the processes of learning that underpin the cultural changes required to support sustainable and resilient communities and the importance of education and training in innovation and sustainability systems. Key emphases include the roles of schools, colleges and universities, as well as adult and community education, in building understanding and capacities in social inclusion, active and informed citizenship, international understanding, sustainable lifestyles and green skills.

10. Social change for sustainability

The challenges of sustainability and climate change involve significant change in the ways that we live, work and interact. This theme explores opportunities to facilitate social change that move beyond the current focus on individual resource consumption and behaviour to consider why and how people produce and consume from broader societal contexts. Sub-themes and concepts include; sharing economies, beyond behaviour change, sustainable consumption, de-growth and affluenza.

11. Green economy transitions

This theme emphasizes equity and justice in regional transitions to a low-carbon economy. This theme also focuses on the governance and management of transitions in social and economic development infrastructure systems and the policies and practices required for an equitable, just and low-carbon future.

12. Sustainable business practices

Sustainable logistics and supply chain management are fundamental to sustainable cities. This theme investigates these and related issues such as sustainable procurement, sustainability indicators and reporting, ethical governance and finance, corporate social responsibility, and carbon accounting and management.

13. Social innovation

The concept of social innovation describes a new approach to solving a shared problem or unmet demand where the returns or benefits of the innovation are realized at the social rather than individual level. Where the classic formulation of innovation focuses on business entrepreneurship, social innovations involve new processes, technologies or institutional partnerships that advance human needs and capabilities.

Chapter 3: Trends Driving Greener Supply Chains

Many businesses today are seeking smart ways to reduce supply chain waste and carbon impact. Over the next several years, the following trends could transform logistics operations, particularly in emerging markets.

1. Creative, collaborative planning. Logistics providers and shippers can find simple ways to better manage schedule requirements, such as building slow-steaming into overseas shipment planning. Involving marketing and sales staff in supply chain planning can help them understand customer and product demand cycles.

2. Emerging markets and infrastructure. Big improvements will occur in ports, road, and rail across emerging markets. Southeast Asia is moving to cleaner, more efficient trucking: better roads, quicker delivery, higher quality, lower environmental impact, and increased fleet regulation. In the Middle East, too, the trend is toward lower emission, more fuel-efficient vehicles.

3. Industry, government, and civil society working together. The logistics sector is collaborating with organizations such as Business for Social Responsibility, World Resources Institute, and the Greenhouse Gas Protocol to help develop standards for measuring, reporting, and managing

environmental impact in supply chain and logistics operations.

4. Regulations enabling positive change and good business. If instituted holistically and sensibly, regulation can mean a step forward for clean and efficient transport, and a force for change in emerging and developed economies alike. The logistics sector can play a role in crafting and enacting sensible legislation that will enable business, and reduce supply chain environmental impact.

5. Green rail and air initiatives. Developed markets such as Europe and North America will achieve greater efficiency in their rail systems, railways will improve in emerging markets, and electric rail will be used more in logistics. Air freight will remain an important part of the overall transport mix, but shippers will continue to use it judiciously. For example, producers may ship limited volumes of new goods by air to meet initial planned demand, while most of the products ship by ocean to better manage cost and environmental impact.

6. 3D-printing use. Manufacturing and production will rely more on parts and components manufactured locally and on a large scale using robust 3D-printing operations. This may drive more efficient and cleaner inbound logistics operations.

7. E-commerce expectations. e-Bay and Amazon succeeded in managing single-product delivery to consumers' doors and changed customer expectations. The better logistics companies manage

information, the better they will be able to adapt to environmental and resource-driven technology changes.

8. Automated vehicles. In cities, automated vehicles will be used more in last-mile delivery. Automated, GPS-controlled, driverless warehouse vehicle technology will likely undergo rapid development and become more widespread.

9. The move to closed-loop manufacturing. Product end-of-life will gain in importance, with logistics companies being more engaged in managing it. As resources become more costly, recycling and reuse will be recognized as big opportunities for optimization and cost efficiency. Manufacturers will ask for and return a deposit on the products they sell, and will reintegrate returned, used products into the manufacturer's production cycle. Logistics will be a critical enabler of this process.

10. Growing consumer awareness. Consumer awareness of product-specific carbon footprints will increase pressure that results in new regulation.

Chapter 4: Steps to a Greener Supply Chain

They say admitting you have a problem is the first step toward recovery. When it comes to energy usage and waste in supply chains, we have a major problem.

The U.S. Department of Energy's Annual Energy Review shows that industrial and transportation sectors; those that coincide with supply chain activities account for 61 percent of U.S. carbon emissions. This indicates that a careful examination of energy use throughout the supply chain provides substantial opportunities for improvement. Volatile energy costs substantially drain company resources. New government regulations will require companies to cut energy use or pay penalties. Pressure from customers, shareholders, and advocacy groups continues to mount for companies to cut energy usage and reduce their carbon emissions.

We offer 12 suggestions for how companies can make their supply chains 'greener,' more efficient and more cost effective in this chapter. These apply to virtually any industry; construction, rail, electronics, food and beverage, retail, industrial, consumer packaged goods, etc.

1. Redesign the product

Even simple changes to a product design; from reducing weight to making it easier to disassemble can reduce energy consumption and waste throughout the product life cycle. In some cases, innovation or new technologies may make it possible to eliminate components or ingredients entirely and thereby shorten the supply chain.

2. Reconfigure manufacturing

Streamlining production steps, reducing energy use, and limiting use of pollutants and toxic materials can have a big impact on how green the supply chain is. Employing a product lifecycle management process that takes into account green considerations is the key. Canadian pulp and paper company Catalyst Paper Corporation reduced greenhouse gas emission by 70 percent and saved $4.4 million by reusing waste products and heat from its manufacturing processes and switching to natural gas.

3. Shift to green suppliers

Although some may have higher costs, green suppliers can have a big effect on the carbon implications of bringing products to market. An analysis of alternative suppliers may uncover potential benefits that justify making a change, such as helping you meet new government regulations or appealing to new categories of consumers.

4. Shorter distances

By rationalizing sourcing, assembly and distribution in relation to markets, travel distances and corresponding fuel use can be reduced. For some products, simply working with suppliers who are closer to major markets can significantly reduce energy use. An American bath and kitchen products manufacturer reduced carbon emissions 34 percent by relocating its warehouses, without incurring additional costs.

5. Alter service-level agreements

When evaluating the effectiveness of your supply chain, add carbon to the traditional measurements of cost, quality and service. Review service-level agreements for unnecessary requirements that decrease efficiency. For example min-max and just-in-time clauses could force suppliers to make small, expedited deliveries that drive up energy use dramatically.

6. Shrink packaging

New materials and designs allow companies to make packages smaller and lighter, allowing shipping containers to hold more and trucks to carry more products in a load. Improved package designs can also reduce the burden of recycling or eliminating packaging materials at the end of the chain.

UK retailer Tesco asked suppliers to provide lighter weight wine bottles, reducing its annual glass usage by 2,600 tons per year and lowering carbon emissions from transportation by 4,100 tons.

7. Plan for reverse supply chain activity

Products that are reclaimed from the market for upgrade, refurbishment, recycling or disposal require some kind of reverse supply chain. This is becoming a business requirement, largely driven by governmental regulation; the European Union adopted product take-back regulations over 7 years ago, and similar statutes are coming online in the U.S. and elsewhere. By planning for these events up front, it's possible to reduce unacceptably high waste and energy costs later. How products are originally designed, assembled, labelled, and packaged can have a profound effect on the efficiency of any reverse supply chain.

8. Consolidate shipments

There is a reason Amazon charges you less for shipping if you consolidate your order and have all items shipped at once; it saves them money. The simple idea of consolidating shipments can require careful analysis to work out which suppliers to use, where to locate facilities, and what inventory levels to maintain.

9. Plan smarter routes

There is an art to planning distribution routes and choosing the right transportation modes. Simple intuition seldom leads to optimal solutions, and over time tradition and inertia often allow routes to settle into patterns that are inefficient and wasteful. Factoring in the true costs and carbon implications can lead to more rational routes. By using a software planning tool that eliminated left-hand turns, UPS was able to take 28.5 million miles off its delivery routes, saving three million gallons of gas and reducing CO2 emissions by 31,000 metric tons per year.

10. Coordinate with partners

Many opportunities to make your supply chain greener or more transparent will depend on careful coordination with allies both upstream and down.

Be prepared to share your goals and plans with these allies and incorporate their plans and priorities into your solutions. British retailer Marks & Spencer worked closely with suppliers to develop a whole new level of transparency; meat used in sandwiches and recipes can be traced back to the individual cow and traceability for clothing reaches as far as dye houses and spinning mills.

11. Take a life-cycle view

Look at the whole life of the product to understand where energy is being used and find opportunities. Energy used while a product is in service can be significant.

A life-cycle assessment by Unilever of its Ben and Jerry's ice cream showed that only 2 percent of its carbon output came from manufacturing; the bulk, 46 percent, came from retail operations such as refrigeration.

12. Start now

The ability to eliminate waste and pollution is becoming an increasingly important criterion for buyers. Making progress reinforces a positive impression of your brand and is a source of pride for employees. For many businesses, mandated changes are inevitable. Start by analyzing which opportunities deserve investment now and which should wait. First, focus on the opportunities you control, then reach out to the opportunities upstream and down in your supply chain.

Chapter 5: Using Optimization to Achieve a Green Supply Chain

"Going Green" is becoming a higher priority for companies large and small, as regulatory bodies and consumers around the world push for more readily-available information on corporate carbon footprints and companies' plans to control / reduce their carbon emissions. But how do you do this most cost-effectively? Optimization is a tool that can lead to better "green" decision-making.

First, let's review of the types of decisions that companies are making today. Here are some real world examples from recent press reports...

Dole Food Company, the world's largest producer of fruits and vegetables, has committed to make its banana and pineapple business in Costa Rica carbon neutral over the next decade. Dole recently highlighted their priorities in achieving this as stated below.
1. Measurement of current carbon footprint and activities, such as the use of fertilizers, research into and collaboration on mitigation and sequestration projects.
2. Improved operations, including increased use of rail transportation on land and more energy-efficient refrigerated containers for maritime shipments.

Tyco Waterworks, a worldwide supplier of water system equipment based in the UK, has documented its consolidation of multiple manufacturing plants into a single Manufacturing Centre of Excellence for meter boxes, plastic injection moulding and gunmetal products in Bridgend, South Wales. Having all its manufacturing under one roof results in a reduction in the company's overall energy consumption and transport, with a resulting positive impact on its carbon footprint (as well as giving operational efficiency benefits.)

Xerox Corporation, which provides document services and equipment around the world, maintains a fleet of 5,000 vehicles used by its technicians in the United States as they respond to customer requests for service. Xerox's manager of programs and operational support, said in an interview that his programs, which have reduced fuel consumption over the last several years by 10%, and have a goal of a 25% reduction, can be grouped into four categories.
1. Pairing each driver with the best-sized vehicle for his / her needs.
2. Improving the fleet's fuel efficiency as vehicles are replaced.
3. Tracking driver routes and distances travelled on a daily basis.
4. Using GPS systems to match available technicians against pending requests as they are dispatched during the day.

The common thread? These companies have made progress towards their cost and carbon goals by.

1. Understanding their current situation, and what their options include.
2. Implementing more efficient operations over their existing supply chain (thus generally using less energy and lowering their footprint).
3. Making the most effective capital additions to their supply chain systems when justified.

Optimization techniques can allow you to identify the best solutions that are possible in improving efficiency and implementing capital projects. Thus you can make the best choices for meeting your goals from the options that you have at hand.

In making decisions for a manufacturing-oriented supply chain like the one described for Tyco Waterworks in this chapter there are tools that can help you evaluate the benefits of.
1. Keeping or consolidating existing facilities, as well as.
2. Opening potential manufacturing sites, taking into account capital costs.
3. Shutdown charges.
4. Manufacturing rates and costs.
5. Freight costs.
6. A host of other costs and constraints on operations.

Xerox and Dole have scheduling problems that can be solved by both optimization and heuristic means. Transportation scheduling problems can be solved; using the technology of the 21st century will be critical for businesses to meet their "green" objectives.

Chapter 6: Cashing in on Your Green Supply Chain Decisions

Supply Chain optimization is a topic of increasing interest today, whether the main intention is to maximize the efficiency of one's global supply chain system or to pro-actively make it greener. There are many changes that can be made to improve the performance of a supply chain, ranging from where materials are purchased, the types of materials purchased, how those materials get to you, how your products are distributed, and many more. An additional question on the mind of some decision makers is. Can I minimize my environmental footprint and improve my profits at the same time?

Many changes you make to your supply chain could either intentionally or unintentionally make it greener, so effectively reducing the carbon footprint of the product or material at the point that it arrives at your receiving bay. Under the right circumstances, if the reduced carbon footprint results from a conscious decision you make and involves a change from 'the way things were', then there might be an opportunity to capture some financial value from that decision in the form of Greenhouse Gas (GHG) emission credits, even when these emission reductions occur at a facility other than yours.

As an example, let's consider the possible implications of changes in the transportation component of the footprint and decisions that might allow for the creation of additional value in the form of GHG emission credits. In simple terms, credits might be earned if overall fuel usage is reduced by making changes to the trucks or their operation, such as the type of lubricant, wheel width, idling elimination (where it is not mandated), minimizing empty trips, switching from trucks to rail or water transport, using only trucks with pre-defined retrofit packages, using only hybrid trucks for local transportation and insisting on ocean going vessels having certain fuel economy improvement strategies installed. These are just some of the ways fuel can be saved. If, as a result of your decisions or choices made, the total amount of fuel and emissions is reduced, then valuable emission credits could be earned. It is worth noting that capturing those credits is dependent on following mandated requirements and gaining approval for the project.)

If your corporate environmental strategy requires that you retain ownership of these reductions, then you keep the credits created and the value of those credits should be placed on the balance sheet as a Capital Asset. Alternatively, if you are able, the credits can be sold on the open market and the cash realized and placed on the balance sheet. Either way, shareholders will not only get the 'feel good' benefit of the environmental improvement, but also the financial benefit from improvement to the balance sheet. If preferred, the credits can be sold to directly offset the purchase price of the material involved, effectively reducing that price and so increasing the margin on the sales price of the end-product and again improving the bottom line. If capital investment is required as part of the supply chain optimization, the credit value can also be a way to shorten the payback period and improve the ROI, or to allow an optimization to occur

So, when you consider improving your environmental impact or optimizing your supply chain, consider the possibility that there might be additional value to unlock if you include both environmental and traditional business variables in your supply chain improvement efforts.

Chapter 7: How to Make Your Supply Chain More Eco-Conscious

If Earth Day has you thinking about making your supply chain more environmentally sustainable, consider the success of Green Toys, a company that produces toys for tots made in the U.S. from 100 percent recyclable materials.

Started in 2007 as a niche brand, Green Toys has turned into a global company with products sold in over 75 countries. The company sells through retailers, including Whole Foods, Pottery Barn and Barnes & Noble.

When Laurie Hyman was unable to find environmentally sustainable, U.S. made, non-toxic toys for her two children, she and von Goeben teamed up and launched Green Toys to meet that need. The Mill Valley, California based manufacturer makes toys out of recycled milk jugs.

The key to selling a green product is not asking customers to sacrifice quality, says von Goeben. "You pull people in by the utility of the product, whatever its main purpose is. Everything else is nice to have," he says. "If you can give somebody a toy that is the right price, fun and safe and is green and made in the U.S.A. you have a winner."

Here is how Green Toys "greened" its business production.

1. Minimize transportation miles. The production of many goods involves shipping raw materials to China and then shipping the finished product back to the U.S. One of the most energy-saving decisions Green Toys has made is to have its manufacturing facility in San Leandro, California, down the road from its warehouse in Mill Valley, California. "We chose our manufacturer by proximity using Google Maps," says von Goeben.

2. Choose a material you can prove is sustainable. Green Toys products are made out of used milk jugs, a product that resonates with customers who have likely used and recycled the jugs themselves.

Once you have identified a sustainable material, be transparent with your customers about your production process and the environmental savings, says von Goeben. "We don't have this locked gate around our process," he says. Being open about how its production process is saving the environment engenders trust among its consumers, he says. Green Toys also makes easy-to-read info-graphics to illustrate how much energy is saved for every pound of recycled milk jug plastic that is used instead of non-recycled plastic.

3. Look for new sources of recycled material. Finding a competitive source for a recycled material requires research and comparison shopping, says von Goeben. But a good place to start is at national associations for

those industries. For example, consult The Association of Postconsumer Plastic Recyclers to find plastic processors.

Bales of recycled milk jugs are sold to processors that turn the jugs into tiny pellets, which Green Toys buys 50,000 pounds at a time and stores in a silo, large storage bins. In the early days, Green Toys rented silo space to hold the pellets, but it now has one of its own. "The day we got our own silo was a really big deal to us," von Goeben says.

4. Design your product to fit the recycled material. A toy manufacturer using virgin, or non-recycled, plastic does not have the same design requirements that a Green Toys product does. To be able to produce a product that is completely made out of 100 percent recycled material, von Goeben and Hyman needed to design a product with no paint, no screws, no glue and no metal. The solution? Sections of the toys fit together puzzle-style.

5. Don't forget to green your packaging. If you are not ready to "green" your entire supply chain, take a look at your product packaging as a place to start adding sustainability to your business model. Because of its soup-to-nuts sustainability philosophy, the Green Toys products are packed and shipped in corrugated boxes that are themselves 100 percent recyclable. Von Goeben has noticed businesses making small steps, like removing twist ties from their packaging, he says. "Small steps really do matter."

Chapter 8: How to Build Sustainability into Your Supply Chain

Incorporating sustainability into any company's operations is a hefty issue. But it's also an increasingly popular shift to make.

It's an increasing liability to not do it. There are a lot of companies out there, that understand that they won't be leaders within the field but they don't want to be lagers either.

Today's global marketplace is forcing many companies to re-evaluate, reconstruct, and even collaborate their efforts just to keep up with demands of the industry. While many leading supply chains have already dedicated years of research and figures to develop data, initiatives and solutions to the movement that seems to be steering the industry, some are still trying to decide why they should.

The best way to understand the imperativeness of sustainability is to consider the alternative. The opposite of sustainability is being unsustainable, vulnerable. Too often companies have fallen, or been greatly damaged, because of events that have taken place in other parts of their supply chain, not necessarily things in their traditional sphere of control. These events have run the range of environmental (products or materials tainted with toxic chemicals), economic (cost spikes of a feedstock), or social (poor or illegal labour practices by a supplier). Without designing sustainability into the supply chain of the company, the risk of significant adverse impact is high.

For the majority of large top supply chains, the question is not whether there is a shortage of sustainability efforts and programs, but what are the more efficient ways to successfully execute those initiatives. Cutting out travel distance of goods or eliminating a middle-man might make the supply chain more cost-efficient for the business, and also reduces its footprint from shipping. Other companies and smaller supply chains that don't have the financial means to make such an aggressive push towards sustainability can still make gradual steps to take to be more socially, economically, and environmentally responsible.

Building a sustainable company is a task that must be taken on from all sides. The collective and collaborative efforts of the supply chain industry, with the support from the government, is crucial. Combining the innovative alternatives from chains taking a grassroots approach with the advanced research collected by leaders in the field can help you better understand what you can do to improve your company.

1. Start Small

Decreasing your company's global footprint won't happen overnight; so don't fret if your company doesn't show great improvement the next day.

When you take on sustainability, it encompasses so many different issues. So we suggests tackling the smaller issues first. Some of the low-hanging fruits for a lot companies has always been transportation and sourcing efficiency. If you are able to actually manage that, you are able to manage sustainability in a more aggressive way within the company itself.

The way to identify what your smaller issues might be is to take an inventory of everything that you produce. From product design to costs to recycling, in most cases there is always room for your company to be quicker, cleaner, and better.

2. Step back and look at your overall business strategy.

Really holding a microscope to your company's infrastructure will force you to identify and address some nuance problems that perhaps you have been too busy to correct. It's common for companies to hire an outside consulting company to do this task for them, because it's easier for an outsider to take a critical eye to your business than you and pinpoint problem areas.

3. Pick Your Pony

Once you've determined which parts of your business needs the most attention, we suggest prioritizing which one you will tackle first. Focus your attention on these two or three things.

4. Create a Green Team

All the ideas in the world won't mean a thing without someone there to implement them. Moreover, when you've reached this step, you are now in the same boat as many leading supply chains.

Identify your employees who want to take leadership roles in different sections within the company. You have to have your employees as your stakeholders. They are the ones who are going to drive this and keep up the momentum and energy.

This is the perfect opportunity for you to see which of your employees are ready to take on a more prominent position within the company.

But be careful! Make sure that your green team is put together from varying departments within the company, so as not to leave any department short-staffed.

Chapter 9: Application of Supply Chain Sustainability

Supply chain sustainability is a business issue affecting an organization's supply chain or logistics network in terms of environmental, risk, and waste costs. There is a growing need for integrating environmentally sound choices into supply-chain management. Sustainability in the supply chain is increasingly seen among high-level executives as essential to delivering long-term profitability and has replaced monetary cost, value, and speed as the dominant topic of discussion among purchasing and supply professionals. A sustainable supply chain seizes value creation opportunities and offers significant competitive advantages for early adopters and process innovators.

Supply chains are critical links that connect an organization's inputs to its outputs. Traditional challenges have included lowering costs, ensuring just-in-time delivery, and shrinking transportation times to allow better reaction to business challenges; however, the increasing environmental costs of these networks and growing consumer pressure for eco-friendly products has led many organizations to look at supply chain sustainability as a new measure of profitable logistics management. This shift is reflected by an understanding that sustainable supply chains frequently mean profitable supply chains.

Many companies are limited to measuring the sustainability of their own business operations and are unable to extend this evaluation to their suppliers and customers. This makes determining their true environmental costs highly challenging and reduces their ability to remove waste from the supply chains; however much progress has been made in defining supply chain sustainability and benchmarking tools are now available that enable sustainability action plans to be developed and implemented.

One of the key requirements of successful sustainable supply chains is collaboration. The practice of collaboration such as sharing distribution to reduce waste by ensuring that half-empty vehicles do not get sent out and that deliveries to the same address are on the same truck is not widespread because many companies fear a loss of commercial control by working with others. Investment in alternative modes of transportation such as use of canals and airships can play an important role in helping companies reduce the cost and environmental impact of their deliveries.

Lets' look at ranking system for the different levels of sustainability being achieved by organization.

1. Getting the basics right

This is the base level and is the stage in which the majority of organizations are at. Companies employ simple measures such as switching lights and PCs off when left idle, recycling paper, and using greener forms of travel with the purpose of reducing the day-to-day carbon footprint. Some companies also employ self-service technologies such as centralized procurement and teleconferencing.

2. Learning to think sustainably

This is the second level, where companies begin to realize the need to embed sustainability into supply chain operations. Companies tend to achieve this level when they assess their impact across a local range of operations. In terms of the supply chain, this could involve supplier management, product design, manufacturing rationalization, and distribution optimization.

3. The science of sustainability

The third tier of supply chain sustainability uses auditing and benchmarks to provide a framework for governing sustainable supply chain operations. This gives clarity around the environmental impact of adjustments to supply chain agility, flexibility, and cost in the supply chain network. Moving towards this level means being driven by the current climate (in which companies recognize cost savings through green operations as being significant) as well as pushing emerging regulations and standards at both an industry and governmental level.

Companies looking to implement sustainable strategies down its supply chain should also look upstream. To elaborate, if a company is able to choose between various suppliers, it can for example use its purchasing power to get its suppliers in compliance with its green supply chain standards. In managing suppliers, companies must measure that inputs from suppliers are of high quality, and the usage of water and energy is minimised leading to less pollution, defects and over production. They also must audit their supplier base and make sure that they are improving the supply chain metrics.

Chapter 10: Developing a Sustainable Supply Chain Strategy

These days, you would be hard pressed to find a major global company that isn't pursuing sustainability initiatives. Few lack a strategy for reducing greenhouse-gas emissions, for example. Indeed, thanks to mounting pressure from regulators, consumers and their own employees and shareholders, more and more companies worldwide are starting to provide evidence of a shrinking carbon footprint.

Most companies also recognize that compliance with emissions reporting requirements is just one aspect of more responsible environmental and social stewardship. Many are as keen to demonstrate their commitment to community recycling projects, or human and labour rights, as they are to show that they are responding to the challenge of climate change and small wonder. With energy costs soaring, risks of all kinds on the rise and shortages of even basic natural resources such as water, companies need to take as broad a view of sustainability as possible.

But how can you be truly sustainable if your suppliers; the raw materials producers, component providers, transport and logistics services, and other interconnected businesses that constitute the supply chain are not?

Supply chain officers can fundamentally rethink their role in a sustainable organization. The supply chain, after all, accounts for between 50 percent and 70 percent of both total expenses and greenhouse-gas emissions for most manufacturing companies. Our experience suggests that both manufacturers and retailers, for example, commonly spend at least half of their revenues on raw materials and packaging. A 2010 report from the US Environmental Protection Agency observes that for many sectors of American industry, more than three-quarters of greenhouse-gas emissions originate in the supply chain.

Supply chains, moreover, can be frighteningly fragile. As they have been extended in response to globalization, they have also become increasingly vulnerable to natural disasters, civil conflict and many other common risks. Just consider the impact of the 2011 floods in Thailand, where roughly a quarter of the world's personal computer hard drives are made. Global prices jumped by 28 percent.

Most companies now recognize that a sustainable supply chain is no longer just an optional nice-to-have; it's a business imperative, critical to the success of the organization as a whole in a perilous world. In 2010, a survey of more than 700 members of the United Nations Global Compact on sustainable business practices, shows 96 percent of CEOs says that sustainability should be integrated into all aspects of strategy and operations and 88 percent of them singled out the supply chain as an area of specific importance. Companies don't yet use a common measure for their carbon emissions.

Yet only 54 percent of those CEOs affirmed that they had actually achieved supply chain sustainability. Other evidence strongly suggests that their suppliers are still serious sustainability laggards.

To be sure, these players are starting to disclose their greenhouse-gas emissions. Some 44 percent of the suppliers to the 50 member companies of the independent, non-profit, United Kingdom-based Carbon Disclosure Project (CDP) supply chain program responded to its annual information request last year, for example; only 28 percent of those suppliers said they had actually achieved a reduction in emissions a poor showing compared with the 43 percent of their end customers that had reduced greenhouse-gas emissions.

Quantifying the benefits

Companies can do much more to motivate their suppliers. They could start by helping them quantify the financial, reputational and risk management benefits of a sustainable supply chain; something that fewer than 25 percent of CDP supply chain program member companies currently do.

Developing mechanisms that can capture and calculate all of those benefits; let alone share them with suppliers is certainly a challenge, to say nothing of a considerable added cost. Companies don't yet use a common measure for their carbon emissions, for example. Some report absolute, or overall, emissions year-on-year; others reckon that intensity levels, which measure carbon emissions per unit of product or sales, are more appropriate.

Leading players know that sustainable sourcing has to encompass all elements of the supply chain.

Furthermore, although the reporting of direct and some indirect (so-called Scope 1 and 2, respectively) emissions is now commonplace, a protocol for Scope 3 emissions; which encompass all indirect emissions not included in Scope 2 that occur in the entire business value chain was only recently published by the World Resources Institute, an independent think tank based in Washington, D.C., and the World Business Council for Sustainable Development. To date, few companies use it.

The benefits of engaging suppliers in managing sustainability are just too significant to ignore. Almost 40 percent of CDP members report that they have realized financial savings from their emissions reduction activities, for example, while more than a third have benefited from new revenue streams or, indeed, from savings gained as a result of their suppliers' carbon reduction activities.

When it comes to individual experiences, the benefits can be even more striking. Witness, for instance, how much a leading beverage company saved in both fuel consumption and $CO2$ emissions; more than 1.4 million litres and 3,900 tons, respectively, in 2010 alone when it boosted the efficiency of its truck fleet by engaging in a shared logistics exercise with other companies.

Chapter 11: A Comprehensive Strategy

Leading organizations are clearly forging ahead, with supply chain sustainability despite the measurement challenges and our experience suggests that those with a dedicated and comprehensive strategy across governance, processes and data are more likely to engage successfully with their suppliers. Such players, in fact, achieve supply chain sustainability in three specific ways.

1. Evolving procurement strategies and a cross-functional approach.

Leading companies recognize that procurement plays a key role in any effort to achieve a sustainable supply chain. For instance, 39 percent of corporate members and 28 percent of their suppliers told the Carbon Disclosure Project that they have seen cost savings as a result of having embedded sustainability practices into the procurement function and fully 63 percent of CDP supply chain program members are now training their procurement staff in supply chain carbon management; more than twice as many as in 2009.

The Clorox Co., in fact, aims to embed environmental sustainability into all of the company's core business processes, from product supply and manufacturing through R&D to procurement. The company's environmental sustainability office works with each business to develop a list of annual commitments.

Leading players know, too, that sustainable sourcing has to encompass all elements of the supply chain. At Unilever, for example, sustainability is integral to the company's core business strategy. It enjoys the kind of C-suite commitment essential for strong governance, and is recognized right across the organization as a key enhancer of long-term brand equity. The result: Unilever aims to source 75 percent of paper and board for packaging, all palm oil and half of agricultural raw materials sustainably by the end of 2015.

What's more, 39 percent of CDP supply chain project members say that if suppliers fail to adopt sustainable practices, they will no longer do business with them. Apple, for example, conducts rigorous on-site audits to ensure that suppliers comply with its code of conduct and if a violation is unearthed, the facility has to remedy it immediately and implement a preventive action plan within 90 days.

2. Moving from compliance to performance improvement

Sustainability, of course, needs to be much more than a box-ticking exercise; though many companies still appear to believe that simply communicating their carbon management information to the outside of the world will suffice.

The leaders, however, are starting to move beyond sustainability as merely a compliance issue, or even an exercise in risk management. They actually identify opportunities for business improvement; a strategy that is more than twice as likely to bring their suppliers onboard, according to a recent research.

Indeed, such efforts can generate significant business value for suppliers. Consider, for example, how Wal-Mart helped several of its supplier apparel mills in China undergo onsite energy assessments, which allowed one, Dana Undies, to identify and implement energy-efficient practices that cut more than 70 percent from its annual energy bill. Or witness how Tata Steel encourages entrepreneurs from disadvantaged communities in India to become suppliers through a combination of local training initiatives and help with working capital, as well as by giving them preference over larger multinationals, providing certain standards are met.

Nestle, meanwhile, is engaging with the farmers who provide the bulk of its raw materials to share best practices and drive innovations that have significantly improved their lives.

3. Building on communications for better decision making.

Most companies are drowning in sustainability-related data, but few are actually mining it for the rich insights that can drive better decision making for themselves and their suppliers. Leading organizations, by contrast, recognize that information management is key to successfully achieving a sustainable supply chain and they are investing in the development of information management platforms that can integrate with their own existing databases to enable more efficient information exchange.

These initiatives take different forms. But they are all aiming toward the same goal; better communications with suppliers in the interests of improving sustainability performance right across the supply chain.

As businesses move toward sustainability as a driver of competitive advantage and higher performance, they will need to develop even more collaborative and cross-functional supply chain teams. They will also benefit from exploring new business models with their suppliers, including opportunities for co-branding. They will need to continue to develop sophisticated new tools to measure and allocate the gains from sustainable practices among the supply chain's stakeholders quantification techniques that allow users to value entire business ecosystems and include sustainability in assessing the total cost of an economic activity.

The disparate contributors to greenhouse-gas emissions in the supply chain are slowly converging on common sustainability standards. But companies remain split on which measure absolute or intensity-based; more accurately quantifies CO_2 emissions.

Clearly, there need to be a balance. Absolute reduction targets might appear most desirable; global warming, after all, will continue, no matter how much emissions per unit of product sold decline, if only because companies will go on making more product. But it's important to recognize that organizations can also meet such targets by divesting emissions-intensive operations or by outsourcing always, of course, paying special attention to the impact of such a move on the overall supply chain.

Much, in short, remains to be done before supply chain sustainability becomes more widespread across both industries and geographies. In the meantime, the business case for it is indisputable. By collaborating with their suppliers to drive mutual benefits, leading companies are making significant headway toward its achievement.

Chapter 12: Collaborating for Better Information Management

Learning from others by sharing information can help any organization. When it comes to developing a sustainable supply chain, such a strategy can be critical especially as research shows that companies still struggle to persuade their suppliers that sustainability makes sound business sense.

Many companies are joining forces with their suppliers in a variety of information management initiatives designed to encourage collaboration and the effective exchange of relevant sustainability information. As a result, the participating parties are not only eliminating redundancy multiple stakeholders requesting the same information reducing costs and managing risk better. Suppliers are also gaining strategic advantages preferred vendor status among them.

Take, for example, the Carbon Disclosure Project supply chain program, an initiative launched in 2007 as part of the independent, non-profit CDP's program to collect data on corporate greenhouse-gas emissions. The project provides a global process for disclosing carbon emissions along the supply chain by enabling its 50 members to engage better with suppliers on the measurement and management of their emissions. Among the participants is Anglo-Dutch consumer packaged goods giant Reckitt Benckiser, which in 2012 exceeded its goal of reducing carbon emissions by 20 percent; by a full percentage point and eight years ahead of time.

Meanwhile, the Supplier Ethical Data Exchange, known as Sedex, provides the secure exchange of sustainability information for more than 25,000 suppliers and their customers worldwide via an online database that allows members to store, share and report on sustainability information, including self-assessed and third-party social audit results. Paris-based EcoVadis is used by several thousand global companies to assess the environmental and social performance of their suppliers by using simple and reliable suppliers' scorecards, covering 150 purchasing categories and 21 corporate social responsibility criteria.

Some of these exchange platforms are industry-specific. The New York-based Fair Factories Clearinghouse, for example, provides its members with the technology to share ideas about how to improve conditions in their plants and factories globally. It was set up in the United States by the National Retail Federation, and Reebok International in particular, as well as the Retail Council of Canada and World Monitors, a New York-based consulting group committed to aligning business practices with human rights.

Brussels-based COCIR, meanwhile, brings together the constituent companies of Europe's healthcare IT, electro-medical and radiological industry, and helps them develop responses to evolving sustainability standards.

Chapter 13: Share Sustainability Best Practices with Suppliers

Driven by a desire to gain a better knowledge and understanding of its supply chain, Nestlé, the Switzerland-based global food company, has developed a procurement procedure that has helped deepen relationships with suppliers on issues ranging from water management and nutrition, right through to using sustainable procurement for rural development.

The Nestlé Supplier Code covers all of the company's suppliers, worldwide and forms an integral part of all purchase orders and supply contracts across every market and business, including the supply of agricultural raw materials a critical area of any food company's supply chain. By applying the code, Nestlé has encouraged best practices in sourcing and has thus helped ensure the long-term supply of safe, quality-assured and regulatory-compliant agricultural materials for its business.

In the dairy sector, for instance, the company has worked with the Swiss College of Agriculture to help develop the Response-Inducing Sustainability Evaluation (RISE), which assesses sustainability holistically across multiple ecological, economic and social dimensions, including energy consumption. The evaluation is based on data collected at the farm level, using a comprehensive questionnaire. Ten key, computer-generated indicators identify potential strengths and weaknesses with regard to sustainability, and Nestlé discusses intervention points for improvement with the farmers themselves.

RISE has not only helped identify opportunities to reduce greenhouse-gas emissions. By simultaneously providing assessment analysis feedback to farmers as the data is collected, the company also stimulates other improvements. Indeed, Nestlé's engagement with its farmers has helped them innovate to enhance the quality of their own lives; just the sort of mutually beneficial outcome that is key to success in the quest for a truly sustainable supply chain.

In China, for example, the company's specialists have trained farmers to handle and store animal manure safely by using biogas digesters, or waste management solutions that trap methane as it is produced. The technology clearly helps reduce greenhouse-gas emissions; but it also makes methane readily available for cooking or even for electricity generation in farming communities.

Thanks to education and outreach programs that have stimulated demand, this technology has been replicated in other countries whose farmers supply Nestlé Indonesia and Mexico among them. In Mexico, for example, 16 industrial biogas digesters have been built in regions that provide more than 35 percent of the milk bought by Nestlé Mexico.

Chapter 14: Why Sustainable Supply Chains Make Business Sense

One may ask; to protect against reputational damage and the effects of climate change, do companies need to implement sustainable business practices throughout their supply chain?

If you were looking to buy a hard drive for your computer around December 2011, you might have noticed prices had been steadily rising since October. But this was no simple case of high-street retailers cashing in on the Christmas rush; the cause was far more complex and revealed much about the vulnerability of global supply chains. The rising prices were a direct result of devastating floods in Thailand, caused months earlier by an unusually severe monsoon season, which in turn was attributed to climate change.

Along with the tragic loss of more than 800 lives, the 2011 Thailand's floods cost the country an estimated $45bn (£28bn). With two of the world's largest hard-drive manufacturers being heavily reliant on Thai suppliers, costs skyrocketed for global companies such as Hitachi, Dell and HP.

The disaster highlighted an increasingly common problem; for any company relying on a global supply chain, the risks facing suppliers on a local level can have a domino effect until damage is felt in boardrooms thousands of miles away. That could be having to raise prices, as was the case with the Thai floods, or it could be reputational damage, such as Apple experienced when it was claimed workers in a Chinese factory, which manufactured some of the company's products, were working in substandard conditions.

So in an increasingly global marketplace, how can businesses ensure their supply chains are resilient to the many risks posed by climate change and the possibilities of unethical practices in distant factories?

We could say one of the biggest issues facing the introduction of more resilient, sustainable supply chains is the quarterly report-dominated thinking of many boardrooms. Speaking off the record, a friend of mine once said it was important for business leaders to focus on the "20-year results" not just on the quarterly results. In other words, long-term resilience is often overlooked due to understandable pressure to focus on short-term profits; however, if sustainability were viewed through the lens of risk to business continuity, the case for a longer-term approach would be easier to make.

The solution starts with ensuring sustainability is understood in the boardroom. A discussion a friend of mine did had with a business leader who disagreed that "making the business more efficient, spending less money on resources and wasting less" were necessarily "sustainable" issues. To the business leader, they were simply "common sense".

This then stressed the need to make the language of sustainability relevant to the boardroom by placing it in context. If businesses are talking about sustainability being in some way separate from the 'day job' ... we won't make the same level of progress as if those roles dissolve into the fabric of the business and it becomes part of people's day jobs.

Making business case for introducing sustainable practices across companies and their supply chains is key. This isn't about trying to sell morality into the boardroom, it's about providing the ability for businesses to make better decisions to reduce costs, improve productivity, support growth and take longer-term decisions. Introducing a more sustainable way of doing business stands a good chance in the boardroom, by focusing on the resource-efficiency agenda.

While many people agreed that focusing on resources would highlight potential financial gains and liabilities, the challenge was finding ways to quantify them on a macro level. In particular, it was felt that identifying the benefits provided by the natural environment, such as fuel, water, climate and land was particularly difficult for companies. eco-system services are not correctly valued by most businesses. Once you have a system to value eco-system services, then the business case for embedding sustainability will be easier.

For example Puma developed an environmental profit and loss approach that tried to work out the true cost of the company's water use, greenhouse gas emissions, land use, air pollution and waste. The 2011 report showed the cost of these services to Puma was about €145m (£125m). If companies knew the true value of these eco-system services they could make better-informed decisions about how to manage their environmental risks. You can't change anything until you've first measured it.

Companies needed to reduce the risk of reputational damage emanating from the supply chain. There is more than one way to create profit. You can create it long term by reducing volatility in your business by saying, we will not walk consciously into a relationship or a contract where we know we are taking on risks that prove to be damaging to our reputation.

So how can companies reduce volatility and introduce sustainable business practices across supply chains?

Larger companies could create a new competitive landscape by moving from "requesting" certain standards from suppliers to "requiring" guidelines to be met. A very positive change could result from saying to suppliers, we have just made a promise and now you are all going to have to go and keep that promise; however, the idea of asking companies to enforce standards across their supply chains was unrealistic at present. Companies need to source competitively priced materials and enforcing standards would result in suppliers raising their prices.

I did spent some time in factories in China, working for big corporates on their supply chains. The fast-moving consumer goods sector likes the sustainability agenda but, at the end of the day, they will say "my suppliers are my biggest asset". Managing suppliers is the critical element. The guys in the factory in China have no interest whatsoever in moral sustainability outcomes unless the customer was prepared to pay a really good margin.

This view was not reflective of all industries, as many businesses were asking suppliers to adhere to certain standards as part of their contracts however; if enough businesses collaborated and all asked their suppliers to take sustainability seriously, those factories would have to change their business models to keep their customers happy.

Government legislation could help in moving the agenda forward and encourage collaboration. Landfill Tax offered a good example in the UK economy of how a tax could transform industry. The Landfill Tax was introduced in 1996 and charges companies and councils for every tonne of material sent to landfill. By making the disposal of waste in landfills more expensive, the government hoped to encourage the development of innovative recycling infrastructure. That is a great example of the right regulation causing collaboration in the supply chain, having a financial incentive, but not having the government writing the blueprint saying 'this is how you have to do it', but instead taking a step back and letting industry take that over.

There was a feeling among some industry experts that while tax would certainly be a driver for change, it was perhaps slightly quixotic to expect such legislation to be implemented on a global scale. A friend of my disagreed, stressing the need for CEOs to lobby governments as it was in their "enlightened self-interest" to do so. "Unless we get real, unless we go and get our leaders to wake up and get strong and passionate about this, we are not going to get anywhere," he said.

Legislation and collaboration across supply chains and among competitors were suggested by many as ways of creating a level playing field so all businesses could be confident of operating in the same commercial environment, which would encourage behavioural change all the way through the supply chain.

The overriding feeling among many industry experts was that the business case for sustainability-focused companies and supply chains was so clear, it had to be a priority in boardrooms. The $45bn cost of the flooding in Thailand and the subsequent rise in the price of hard drives demonstrates the need to take climate change and the effect it will have on business seriously. Let's think about what is good for business and good for countries and make decisions on the back of that. If it's not commercial, it's not sustainable.

Chapter 15: Why Companies Top Struggles Lie in Sustainable Supply Chains

Despite a number of recent government-led and industry-specific initiatives to simplify the process, companies are still struggling to get a grip on their supply chains, according to a recent report by Business for Social Responsibility (BSR), a non-profit that promotes sustainability in business. The report, called the BSR/Globescan State of Sustainable Business Poll 2012, found that the top sustainability challenge for companies was achieving solutions throughout the supply chain.

Nearly 42 percent of the more than 550 professionals polled said ensuring their suppliers followed sustainable practices was the greatest obstacle to achieving their climate sustainability goals.

The results point toward the challenge faced by companies to boost their supplier engagement and bridge the gap between suppliers simply filling out disclosure forms to actively reducing their carbon footprint.

But companies often face a number of obstacles getting to that point. Many companies don't have visibility beyond the first or second tier of their value chains, largely due to the so-called confidentiality of the supply chain. A big retailer like Wal-Mart will buy product from a company, which in turn buys product from another company, which buys from a third or fourth company, and the entire sequence is seen as proprietary. That nature and sense of confidentiality flows down the supply chain, and that is the primary roadblock or challenge.

Sub-contracting is another big issue. In the apparel industry, for example, sub-contracting is standard practice, and many clothing companies therefore can't see beyond the first tier of their value chains. One stitching factory, for instance, may use anywhere from 10 to 15 sub-contractors, without disclosing their identities. Getting visibility all the way out to the cotton fields is something that quite few companies actually have.

Despite these challenges, companies are developing initiatives to combat the issue. Levi Strauss & Co., for example, recently deployed an information-management system that allows the apparel company to collect and track its suppliers' energy use data, as well as simplify the data collection process. Using this new system, Levi's started in 2011 to collect annual water and energy consumption data from more than 60 of its high-volume suppliers. Each supplier received performance feedback and took energy reduction measures where relevant, such as installing energy-efficient lighting in offices or using direct drive sewing machines to improve efficiency. Many of the company's suppliers have reduced their energy use by nearly 30 percent, said a company spokesperson.

Some companies have been spurred into action by the government to examine their supply chains. In

August, the US Securities and Exchange Commission passed a ruling that requires public companies to investigate their supply chains and disclose if their products use tin, tungsten, tantalum or gold from war-stricken Democratic Republic of Congo and surrounding areas. Many leading automakers and electronics companies have created industry-wide coalitions and tools to help make the process easier, and ensure the minerals they use are conflict-free. Recent initiatives include a new web-based tool launched by more than two-dozen auto companies like Ford and Honda that allows companies to request information from each one of their suppliers, or a fund backed by companies such as HP and Intel that lowers the cost for smelters that wish to prove they are conflict-free.

There is no one-size-fits-all solution, each industry requires a different approach. For example, BSR has for a number of years worked with luxury brands that manufacture exotic skin products, such as handbags made from crocodile skin. The industry's supply chain is not organized around corporate lines and so it's especially difficult to track; often a farmer will catch some snakes and in an often haphazard way get the snakes into the hands of a middle man, who in turn sells them to a big brand name. These companies are now exploring the use of DNA testing to find out exactly where their raw materials have come from. But this solution will likely only be effective for certain industries, if any. It's expensive and might be doable; it's hard to do for products that have much lesser value.

The first step to better understanding its supply chain is for a company to find out what makes up its chain; who are its suppliers, where are they based, and if possible, who they are sub-contracting to. Once a company gains a better grasp of its supply chain; solutions will start to emerge.

The BSR poll, which was conducted recently, surveyed companies from around the world, including; Africa, Latin America and the United States.

Other challenges cited by the respondents for achieving climate sustainability include establishing a strategy that will have the greatest impact and gaining resource commitments from senior management. Companies need to accept that they would likely never fully achieve all the sustainability solutions they hope to through their supply chain. Maybe it will be too expensive to get the type of visibility and management of impact that you desire; you will have to accept that it's imperfect.

Chapter 16: The Need to Reduce Your Carbon Footprint

To make progress on environmental issues, organizations must understand that they are part of a larger system; therefore one may ask. What does it take for an organization to get serious about issues like water, energy, and waste in its supply chain?

It starts to get real when people believe these matters are strategic; that they will shape the future of business. I use the word "sustainability" as little as possible because it's so generic; it makes people's eyes glaze over.

To confront these issues practically, you need employees who are innovative; who have the skill and the vision to redesign products, processes, and business models and who understand the business context. Most important, they need to be able to tell a story about why this is a meaningful journey.

If they are stuck in the mind-set (so popular in business schools, unfortunately) that a company exists to maximize return on investment capital, with an emphasis on short-term financial performance, they won't get very far. What I am describing here is a big change in perspective for most companies.

To me, it's Leadership 101. It starts with "Who are we?" and "Why are we here?" In a great book called The Living Company, published in 1997, Arie de

Geus described a study conducted by Shell in the early 1980s of companies that had survived for more than 200 years. What those organizations had in common was an understanding of themselves as a human community first and a machine for making money second.

We have lost a lot of that sense of company as community. But a business is a group of people working together. You can't build a new vision without a strong, community-oriented culture which, by the way, is rare. It sounds good, everybody nods their heads, but the gap between that idea and the way most managers manage is enormous.

Okay one may ask, assume a community-oriented culture. What challenges must be overcome to make a business more holistic from end to end?

The first challenge is to understand the larger system you are in. The second is to learn to work with people you haven't worked with before. Those two skills might seem distinct, but in practice they are interwoven. The system is too complicated for one person to grasp. It crosses too many boundaries, both internal and external.

The third challenge has to do with how you perceive sustainability. They might not say this, but most companies act as if sustainability is about being less bad. There is certainly a need to reduce your carbon footprint. But people don't get excited about incremental changes like that. They need a more ambitious vision.

The environmental movement is a big culprit in this. There has been so much rhetoric about how bad business is that people inside companies feel guilty, and guilty people are not going to do bold things. But that is crazy! Innovation is what good businesses do best. They are all about creating new sources of value. NGOs and governments can't possibly solve these problems alone; business innovation is essential; therefore one may ask if sustainability issues are often supply chain issues. How do you effect change across a supply chain?

First, you focus on the nature of the relationships. In most supply chains, 90% of them are still transactional. If I am a big manufacturer or retailer, I pressure my upstream suppliers to get their costs down. There is very little trust and very little ability to innovate together. That must change, and it is starting to.

Second, you learn to work with NGOs and other non-business entities. They will give you access to expertise that you can't grow fast internally. Water is a classic example. A few years ago, Coca-Cola decided to cut the water used to make a litre of Coke from more than three litres to 2.5 litres. But it was overlooking the 200-plus litres it took to grow the sugar that went into that Coke. The company found that out because it partnered with the World Wildlife Fund, which knew how to analyze the water footprint of the value chain. Coca-Cola now knows the difference between drip-irrigated sugarcane and flood-irrigated sugarcane.

So why do corporations need NGOs?

For credibility, especially in Europe. People don't trust the business-as-usual mind-set for good reason. I don't think it's so different in the U.S. If a credible NGO certifies your product, your brand can gain hugely if you are willing to change your practices. NGOs can also provide knowledge. No business knows what Oxfam knows about the plight of farmers or what WWF knows about biodiversity and watersheds. The best businesses don't just hire the sharpest people; they also keep expanding their expertise by partnering with NGOs that have deeper and broader knowledge.

One may then ask; what role do leaders play in confronting supply chain challenges?

These are all leadership issues. But when I say "leader," I don't necessarily mean the CEO or even bosses in general. You can't possibly source everything sustainably, as Unilever has declared as a 2020 goal, unless you engage thousands and thousands of people around the world. You will need technical innovations, management innovations, process innovations, and cultural innovations. The people who figure those out are leaders, by definition, and most of them won't be senior executives. All the word "lead" means, if you look at its Latin root, is to step across a threshold.

We may ask if leadership ever come from outside the organization?

The answer is obvious a big YES. When someone comes into an organization; a new hire or even a new supplier; he or she will ask, "Why do we do it this way?" The answer is often "Just because." Now, 90% of those habits may be perfectly okay. But 10% are completely dysfunctional, particularly when the world around you is changing. A cool part of sustainability work is uncovering the assumptions that lead people to do things in a way that is out of touch with the company's larger reality.

How do we get the ball rolling inside organizations?

In some cases, it starts when the CEO steps back to reconsider the organization's relationship to the world. Or when people deep in the business discover some problems, collect some data, and then try to find people who have the skills to do something. Gradually, they build up a network of people who are fascinated by the problem and excited about finding a solution. Nothing motivates designers more than being told that something is impossible, like eliminating a toxin that has always been part of a product or process. That started to happen after Nike's first toxicological study of its products and supply chain more than 10 years ago.

The key is not your position; it's your passion, your ability to form networks, and your organizational savvy. This is where young people sometimes run aground; they have got energy and passion but don't have a clue about the culture of the organization or where the natural pockets of power are.

Obviously, if you are talking about operational changes, you need operating managers. Things get a lot more real when you talk about negotiating and writing contracts differently and changing metrics to gauge more-sustainable sources.

Some people says we are coming to the end of the industrial age and that the industrial age was a bubble. What does that mean?

For more than a century, financial historians have used the "bubble" metaphor to explain why smart people act really stupidly together. Inside the bubble, there is a reality, a language. But outside the bubble there is a larger reality that asserts itself eventually and the bubble bursts. If you think of the industrial age as a bubble, then maybe the larger realities (like finite resources) are starting to assert themselves.

Some people think the industrial age is already over; we are now in the information age. But that is a serious misunderstanding. The industrial age has always been punctuated by radical shifts in dominant technologies; the electric light, the automobile. The internet is just the most recent. The industrial age has been the era when machines and machine thinking shaped our lives. Leaders need to imagine life and their businesses outside that bubble, where efficiency, productivity, and the maximization of return on capital are balanced by the imagination, passion, and trust that shape creativity and innovation.

Chapter 17: How Businesses Can Save Our Cities

Addressing the complex problems of the 21st century requires a new solutions toolbox. Innovation will be absolutely essential and business will lead the way; not just in technology, but also in building new models of collaboration that harness leadership and collective problem-solving to drive effective action.

The World Business Council for Sustainable Development Urban Infrastructure Initiative, a groundbreaking program to promote strategic collaboration between cities and business to drive sustainable development, is a great example of this type of innovation. The release of the (Urban Infrastructure Initiative) UII final report, which captures the lessons from few years of work in 10 cities around the world, presents a great opportunity to highlight how leading businesses can drive new collaboration models forward.

With 7 billion city dwellers likely by 2050, creating sustainable cities will be essential if humanity is to address climate change and move toward a sustainable future. It is, of course, thrilling that mayors around the world are showing real leadership and vision on climate change and sustainable development, but even the most advanced cities will say that they cannot do it alone.

In this regard, many cities are missing out on crucial and valuable input because they are not engaging with business early in the planning process to help turn vision into an actionable and cost-effective plan.

Why is business involvement important?

Early engagement leverages the capability of business to identify innovative and cost-effective solutions to complex, cross-cutting urban sustainability challenges. The key infrastructure, technology, services and financing solutions that will enable the sustainable visions of cities are predominantly developed, designed and implemented by the private sector.

I am talking about solutions such as energy efficient buildings, low-carbon mobility, smart infrastructure systems, renewable energy and inclusive business models for universal access to energy and water, to name just a few.

Why is this form of engagement not happening now? While it is true businesses already design, construct and operate infrastructure for (or in) cities, this traditional involvement is actually late in the planning life cycle; after major choices already are locked in. Furthermore, talking about moving engagement earlier in the process brings out a number of perceptional, procedural and institutional barriers that make this nominally difficult.

This is where the Urban Infrastructure Initiative comes in.

The WBCSD and 14 leading member companies have developed a new model that provides an effective process for early strategic engagement between cities and business for sustainable development.

It mobilizes a multidisciplinary team of private sector experts who work directly with city officials to identify solutions to overcome key challenges a city faces in realizing its sustainability vision. The process is conducted at a pre-commercial stage and is kept technology and vendor neutral, maintaining a clear separation from procurement processes.

Testing the new model for efficacy

While it is still early days, cities are already taking forward the solutions and ideas from these innovative collaborations. Yixing, for example, is fast tracking the development of a green transport network for the city, absolutely critical for several cities in China that are experiencing double-digit population growth.

Promoting this type of collaboration, which harnesses city leadership, business innovation and solution delivery, can unlock an enormous win-win opportunity to drive transformational global action on climate change right in line with the Intergovernmental Panel on Climate Change (IPCC) released report on climate change mitigation.

Cities win by getting practical, cost-effective solutions to realize their ambitious sustainability visions. Leading businesses will win through growing the markets for innovative new solutions that will be essential for delivering rapid change.

The WBCSD is holding discussions with the C40 Cities Climate Leadership Group and others about taking forward the intriguing idea of a "C20-C30-C40" collaboration as a platform for transformational action on climate change.

This is a major recommendation of the Oxford Martin Commission for Future Generations to bring together 20 countries, 30 leading businesses and 40 cities to overcome traditional barriers to action through action-focused collaboration.

Chapter 18: The Crucial Role for Business in Sustainable Economy

The world is experiencing a historic shift of economic and political power from the traditional base of industrialized countries to the emerging economies.

By 2050, when the world's population is expected to be about 9 billion, 70 percent of the world's population will live in urban environments, with the great majority living in cities in developing countries.

Urbanization is happening fast and most of it is being poorly managed, putting hundreds of millions of the urban poor in harm's way.

As the economic emergence of developing countries continues, global consumption patterns will become increasingly critical. Global consumption patterns and trends are putting unsustainable and increasing stress on the Earth's ecosystems, the supply of material resources needed for industrial growth, and human social systems and well-being.

The role of business in addressing the problems of urbanization and unsustainable consumption will be important. There is no longer a choice between economic growth and environmental well-being: they are interdependent, and if we do not make sure we have both, we risk ending up with neither; therefore, it is in the best interest of business to provide sustainable solutions to such growing problems. Business need to contribute to the stability of developing countries, minimize risk by proactively addressing socioeconomic and environmental concerns, develop models for working with low-income communities, and recognize the significant business opportunities available in the transition to a sustainable global economy.

Recognizing that business can neither achieve sustainable development nor alleviate poverty by itself. Business, governments and civil society must all transform, as all three strive, with their different accountabilities and capacities, toward the single goal of sustainable human progress.

Chapter 19: A Green Supply Chain Starts in China

As companies work to reduce their carbon footprint, the easiest steps to take are often the closest to home.

Yet for companies with global operations or supply chains, the biggest practical wins are likely to be found in improving energy efficiency of owned and supplier facilities overseas, where they have the ability to multiply impacts across tens, hundreds, or even thousands of sites through relatively simple central coordination.

For companies looking to increase their supply chain's energy efficiency, China is a good place to start, for a number of reasons.
1. China is a top location for energy-intensive manufacturing and a key node of many supply networks.
2. As the number one emitter of greenhouse gases, China is likely to face more regulatory pressure to improve its performance.
3. Due to its size, China is an ideal place to take energy-efficiency programs to scale.

BSR has spent several months helping Wal-Mart establish its supplier energy efficiency program in China, where the company has set a target of improving the energy efficiency of 200 factories by 20 percent over three years period. Working with Wal-Mart, BSR have seen firsthand how initiatives from other countries can be adopted and adapted to the Chinese context.

This is BSR's guide to starting energy efficiency programs at company operations and in company supply chains in China.

First, the Basics of Building a Successful Program Anywhere

Be Flexible. Effective energy-savings programs, particularly for owned operations, often focus on a specific goal but leave significant flexibility for how corporate targets will be met. Rather than taking a strictly top-down approach that regulates specific changes in technology and behaviour, BSR recommends developing an initiative based on strong leadership and a clear mandate for change. This allows internal business units to find their own solutions and strategies for meeting targets.

The need for flexibility and autonomy is even more pronounced when companies deal with suppliers. Companies often have limited visibility into where the most significant energy savings might be in supplier operations. The best approach is therefore to provide specific tools or approaches that suppliers can use to discover and implement customized solutions for themselves.

Focus on the People and Systems, Not Advanced Technology. Companies usually gain more by investing in existing people and systems rather than expensive new technologies. For example, Swire

Beverages, a major Hong Kong-based bottler, has created energy-management committees composed of production, engineering, environmental health and safety (EHS), and facilities managers who meet regularly to explore possible opportunities for reducing waste and increasing the productivity of manufacturing and logistics processes.

Get Buy-in From Senior Management. This is essential to establish a clear direction and goals for people within the company. Many of the most successful initiatives have been started by executives who challenged employees to reduce energy use or carbon emissions, and then charged each department with determining how to do it. In this way, management can solicit opinions from employees and reward those with innovative ideas. Inter-departmental competition can make the process fun and increase employee engagement. These management techniques can turn employees into an asset rather than a barrier to energy efficiency and waste reduction.

Management buy-in is also necessary when working with suppliers, even if they are small factories. In this situation, while you may target facilities or EHS personnel with trainings and tools, the general manager or other central decision-maker should be your direct liaison.

Don't Wait to See the Data Before You Act. Good data can help you justify new programs and is important for evaluating progress toward goals, but program development can be unnecessarily slow if the initial focus is on assessment of current energy usage. During start-up, while you are building the system and processes for data reporting, most information should actually be flowing toward suppliers, in the form of trainings, tools, and ongoing support. With this approach, suppliers are more likely to align with the emphasis on action, which subsequently can be supported by trustworthy reporting.

Managing from Afar

The lack of hands-on operational control can present challenges; especially for companies with a large supplier base. To ensure that your program is creating the right incentives, invest time and resources in designing the appropriate system for reporting, monitoring, verification, and communicating the right message to suppliers.

Here are some tips for an effective supplier program.

1. Clearly communicate goals, progress, and incentives. Demonstrate your own commitment with clear, quantitative expectations, and then work closely with suppliers to monitor and track progress, and share successes and challenges with other relevant stakeholders.

2. Focus on multiple benefits. Energy-saving efforts can provide significant financial returns for suppliers.

3. Emphasize that you are building long-term relationships with suppliers. Suppliers will recognize

the need to be in line with the company's goals and values to maintain the relationship, and with an emphasis on long-term partnership, suppliers can make investments that require a longer payback period.

4. Explore cost-sharing options. In one supplier program, a global furniture firm paid the program and consulting fees, while the factory paid for energy meters.

5. Promote open communication. Frequent and transparent communication on progress is an important way to provide both support and resources, and to collect credible data to verify claims about energy savings and emissions reductions.

What is Special About the Chinese Context?

Many of the lessons from BSR's energy-efficiency work in China are equally valid for other locations, but working with suppliers in China has specific challenges related to the regulatory context, economic incentives, and the availability of technical and financial resources.

When working in China, business leaders should.

1. See the government as not just a regulator but also a resource. The Chinese government has become increasingly proactive in encouraging improvements in energy intensity (amount of energy used per unit of GDP), and the government's new regulatory targets have been accompanied by resources and training

support for manufacturers. Government can also provide advice on project implementation as well as clear direction on how energy-intensity targets are being applied and measured.

2. Watch utility and fuel prices. Currently, water and electricity are heavily subsidized, which limits the return on energy-savings investments. The economic argument for energy efficiency will be stronger when utility prices rise in accordance with government plans. Some cities and provinces are already beginning to test price increases. Be prepared to take advantage of improvements in the economic argument for energy savings, but meanwhile look for other ways to strengthen the business case.

3. Seek financial help. Many sources provide financial help for energy-efficiency investments, including local governments, energy service companies (ESCOs), the Hong Kong Productivity Council, the International Finance Corporation's China Utility-Based Energy Efficiency Program, the P2E2 program (a partnership between the U.S. Environmental Protection Agency and China's State Environmental Protection Administration), and international and local banks.

4. Use ESCOs to fill knowledge gaps. The ESCO market in China is young but growing rapidly, with both domestic and foreign service providers offering a range of consulting and project management services. Some cheap, do-it-yourself methods such as installing energy meters can create useful data to help suppliers understand where the energy savings opportunities lie, so they can make an informed

decision about when to call for external consulting expertise. BSR has also been working with ESCOs to provide low-cost technical training sessions for factory managers, as consultants are often willing to share basic information and tips on energy management at supplier forums and workshops.

Work on energy efficiency in China has been gradually building for a few years, and it is now expanding rapidly as an increasing number of global companies endeavour to improve supplier performance along with their own environmental impacts. This presents a real opportunity for global companies with operations and supply chains in China to make a bigger impact in emissions reduction.

Chapter 20: Supply Chain Sustainability in Africa

If most industries in Africa embraced the philosophy of reverse logistics on their wastes, new industries, new jobs and new products would spring up from the utilization of recyclable materials.

The key to selling a green product is not asking customers to sacrifice quality, If you can give customers a product that is at the right price, great quality, safe and is green (made from recycled materials) and made in Africa, you would be making an enviable impact in development as well as revenue generation and job creation.

Here are five steps to apply to your business processes to make it greener and more environmentally friendly:

1. Minimize transportation miles.

The production of many goods in Africa has encouraged the habit of shipping or importing raw materials that can be sourced locally, from far away Asia and Europe. A large percentage of these raw materials can be also be found in Africa. There are several instances where a country is importing raw materials which can be found in neighbouring African countries but would prefer to import from across continents. This happens for several reasons one of those being, inadequate security on transport modes or poor road or rail network across countries which eventually raises the costs of the goods. It is important that where some of these inhibiting factors are fair enough or manageable, your business model takes advantage of them by buying/selling the raw materials from/to your next door neighbours.

2. Choose a material that is sustainable.

Let's face it recycling is not a very catchy term yet amongst most parts of Africa, but you cannot deny that people are learning the practice fast with the aim to survive and not necessarily save the environment. This is why it is important you choose a sustainable material that would be easy to find and always in circulation.

A good example is the scrap dealers in Nigeria most of whom have never been to school. You will find these buyers pushing their trolleys ready to buy your non-functional pressing irons, burnt copper coils, cooking plates, non-functioning automobile engines and non-functioning electric generators. They buy these items directly from consumers which makes these items valuable to consumers even when they are not functional, hence consumers would keep them till the scrap dealers come calling. Now these items are taken by the scrap dealers to a sorting and scaling point, weighed and bought by bigger buyers who melt them into iron rods or other reusable items.

3. Keep looking for new sources of recycling material.

Finding a competitive source for a recycled material requires research and comparison shopping. But a good place to start is at national associations for those industries. For example, you can consult your local Association of Post consumer Plastic Recyclers to find plastic processors. You could also find sources of these materials through their agents of consumption or use. For example contacting the Association of Fruit Juice sellers or Association of Party Planners and providing them the offer of cleaning out disposed Tetra packs, disposed drinking water bags and their likes would prove mutually beneficial in the sense that they would have cleaner floor after events and you will have the materials you need.

4. Design your product to fit the recycled material.

A Plastic bag manufacturer using virgin, or non-recycled, plastic does not have the same design requirements that a Green Supply Chain demands. To get your factory to be more environmentally friendly, you must be able to produce a product that is completely made out of 100 percent recycled material. Your end product should be designed in such a way that it is ready or almost ready to be recycled again to give the same product.

5. Don't forget to green your packaging.

If you are not ready to "green" your entire supply chain, take a look at your product packaging as a place to start adding sustainability to your business model. Practice the soup-to-nuts sustainability philosophy, ensure your products are packed and shipped in packaging that are 100 percent recyclable.

Chapter 21: Hong Kong Sustainability Urban Growth

When it comes to sustainable urban growth, Hong Kong has been a noted success story and possible model for mainland China and other emerging economies. The city's emphasis on infrastructure has been its traditional path to development, with new towns and a mass transit railway in the 1970s and 1980s, airport and seaport development in the 1990s, and increased bridge and rail links to mainland China in the 2000s. Hong Kong has also enjoyed the flexibility to experiment with greener, socially conscious, and more sustainable development at its own pace.

Will Hong Kong remain a positive example of sustainable urban growth?

Hong Kong at a glance

1. Constraint: 70 percent of total territory (1,100 square kilometres) is mountains; only 20 percent is available for urban development.

2. Demographic change: The number of births in Hong Kong by mainland China mothers increased by 52 percent from 2006 to 2010.

3. Public trust: The 2012 Edelman Trust Barometer highlights that Hong Kong residents trust business significantly less than NGOs and government. NGOs are the most trusted institutions.

Growing population, high density

Hong Kong's current population of 7.07 million is projected to grow to 8.47 million by 2041, with most of the city's "suburban sprawl" taking place in the densely populated New Territories to the north of the older Hong Kong Island and Kowloon districts. According to experts; the increasing population is happening slowly, not from growing Hong Kong families, which have traditionally been small, but from expatriates and mainland Chinese residents moving to the city.

Hong Kong is more efficient than most of North America Cities due to its high density, something that has also given the city a high ranking on many international city-level sustainability indexes, which typically put a high value on population density. But the high density creates other sustainability challenges related to infrastructure and social issues. Land is scarce, and there is an increased need for both transportation and housing projects.

Currently, however, city planning is not centred on these social needs. For instance, while much of the space planning is done to accommodate cars, only 7 percent of people in Hong Kong own a car. Transportation infrastructure (such as roads and parking) account for 4 percent of the total Hong Kong area, but residential development accounts for only 3 percent of area.

To remedy this challenge, Civic Exchange, a Hong Kong-based sustainability think tank, has begun developing a new City Well-Being Index that takes into account issues Asian urban residents themselves identify as their priorities though engagement (the group has also published a compendium of 160 global city indexes in its 2012 report "Measuring Well-Being in Cities").

Today, one of Hong Kong's biggest sustainability issues is poor air quality. The Hedley Environmental Index, an online air-quality-monitoring tool managed by a group of stakeholders including the Hong Kong University School of Public Health, communicates the health impacts in terms of real-time economic losses. Contrary to casual assumptions given the city's proximity to the manufacturing centres of mainland China, 53 percent of air pollution is generated locally.

One of the primary causes relates to lack of infrastructure planning: Poor airflow through "building canyons"; those high-rise monoliths developed to satisfy housing demand means air pollution becomes trapped. The protests against this type of design have prompted proposed regulation requiring air-circulation studies for new buildings. Another major contributor to poor air quality comes from shipping emissions at the port.

While private-sector developers have started to engage because of new ad hoc regulations and public interest, government appears to be lagging. Hong Kong's air-quality standards are cited by many stakeholders as lax and lacking ambition. When Hong

Kong released its new ambient air-quality standards recently, just two days after Beijing released more ambitious targets for China, concerns about Hong Kong's lack of leadership were exacerbated.

Water is another significant issue that may threaten sustainable growth. With 80 percent of Hong Kong's water coming from the Dongjiang River, projections are dim. Upstream water quality is degrading due to open garbage disposal and untreated waste water surrounding the water supply.

While Hong Kong is currently using less than the allocated limit set by the Guangdong province People's Government, demand is catching up to supply. Additionally, the significant demand from the other cities upstream in the province is set to increase, which could affect availability and price. The one area of success and continued opportunity is in toilet water, for which the city already uses a separate seawater system.

The role of stakeholder engagement

Addressing these challenges and ensuring sustainable growth will require engagement among the government, private sector, and civil society. But due to changing demographics, stakeholder engagement has become contentious, highlighting the question of whether the current model of engagement between government, business, and civil society is achieving the intended benefits.

The Hong Kong government seems to be singularly weak at engaging either with businesses or the civil sector; leading to suspicion and a current impasse. Getting beyond the suspicion is needed to deal with the larger challenges, such as tackling air quality or the growing wealth gap in the population.

Singapore, with its similarly constrained geography, is often held up as a benchmark for Hong Kong. In Singapore, "Sustainability Systems Integration Model" was used. Breaks down sustainability issues into small chunks, allowing for engagement with the right stakeholders, and then re-integration in the city's strategic plan. We believes it has allowed the government to move rhetoric to real engagement.

A consequence of not engaging in sustainable development is the exodus of Hong Kong's inhabitants including Chinese and expatriates working for multinational companies to places like Singapore, where quality of life is ranked comparable or higher. Companies are recognizing that they can attract talent with the offer of a cleaner living environment, more green space, and a more forward-thinking approach to urban development.

Glimmers of success

While the challenges in Hong Kong are growing, there have been successes. MTR Corporation, Hong Kong's first privatized rail and metro company, has thrived by integrating railway infrastructure with urban development. Rather than relying solely on advertisements and fares from riders, the company has worked with government to plan rail systems and stations in conjunction with other properties in the vicinity, including shopping malls, residential towers, office spaces, and hotels. MTR's ability to develop this real estate has allowed it to thrive as a transit system.

A similar example in government transportation policy that took a holistic approach. "The Octopus Card," an IT-enabled smart payment card, can be used for fares and retail purchases, it has transformed public transportation in Hong Kong through intermodal transport and consumer purchases.

Another example of progress is the voluntary business initiative the Fair Winds Charter, which encourages ocean carriers to switch to lower-sulphur fuels while at the port. The initiative has evolved into a public-private partnership, with the government lowering port fees for participating companies. While the initiative will need sustained political will to keep going (there are some doubts if that will happen amid government red tape), the scheme is a model for collaboration among NGOs, government, and business.

Swire Properties, one of Hong Kong's largest developers, is at the centre of the city's challenges and opportunities. According to Cary Chan, Swire's general manager of technical services and sustainability, when operating in one of Asia's most dynamic cities, "It's always challenging to strike a balance between economic development and the environmental impact." Despite this, Swire Properties sees the business value of undertaking efforts to improve energy, air, and water impacts.

"There is an increasing appreciation from our tenants to be more environmentally friendly and transparent," he added. "They also turn to us for sustainable practices to enhance their businesses." In 2008, the company became the first Hong Kong property developer to provide free energy audits for office tenants.

Swire is also making engagement an important part of its strategy, participating in initiatives with government and industry to lead change, using its portfolio as a "living laboratory" to measure the environmental impact of buildings and promote a more integrated design approach.

This type of public awareness, supported by business, could change political priorities to accelerate the adoption of existing technologies for energy efficiency.

Hong Kong has historically lacked the political will and public commitment to embrace energy efficiency. Electricity prices are low by global standards, and pale in comparison to the price of land. This weakens the case for building energy efficiency. But that may be changing. People are starting to connect the dots between energy use and air quality, given the predominance of coal in Hong Kong's electricity fuel supply. Everyone wants cleaner air.

Projected electricity tariff hikes will increase the financial reward for energy efficiency, and the government's new demand-side management to curb energy use should also have a positive effect.

Frankly, Hong Kong has the money, the technology, and the intellectual capital to become the greenest city in Asia. What the city need now is a sense of urgency, unity of purpose, and political capital, to achieve it.

A Holistic Approach

On paper, the city's approach to incorporating sustainability considerations into development; its environmental impact assessment looks sound and has been cited as a leading example of mitigating potential environmental impacts. But it has also been criticized for neglecting to consider social issues and for failing to look beyond a single project at system-wide or regional planning.

Private sector must take a more holistic view to address these gaps. The Corporate social responsibility (CSR) models that companies use in Hong Kong is different from the CSR model that companies use in the West. The needed shift from philanthropy and community giving to one that recognizes the strategic aspects of CSR.

It is also striking that most conversations about Hong Kong's infrastructure development completely ignore what will happen in 2047, when the "one country, two systems" approach will end. The implied uncertainly should affect long-term decisions, given that planning for basic infrastructure for transportation, water, and energy is likely to cover this time frame and beyond.

Given what has worked in Hong Kong and the looming challenges the city faces, the private sector is well-positioned to provide leadership in creating a more holistic view. When business engages proactively with stakeholders, rather than waiting for government directives, it can decipher the operating environment in ways that highlight opportunities, manage trade-offs, and make the business case for more sustainable infrastructure development. In the case of Hong Kong, sustainable development must be led by new business models that may be achieved by stepping out with broader insights from a wider set of stakeholders.

A Tale of Two Possible Cities

Many of the right pieces seem to be in place for making Hong Kong a sustainability success story; an engaged and educated population, financial success, population density to create economies of scale, and access to advanced and efficient technologies.

Hong Kong may be a model for sustainable growth, but it will first need to deal with looming questions and attainable opportunities. There may be two routes for this city in flux; one that clings to past glory and fails to mobilize in new, collaborative ways, or one that looks inward and finds the political will to address the potentially runaway demographics. The latter path will require meaningful stakeholder engagement between government, civil society and the private sector to dig out of a deepening lack of trust, and put the city squarely on the path to sustainable growth.

Chapter 22: The Rapid Development of Dubai

Since 1950, Dubai population grew about 100 times from a small town of 20 thousands inhabitants to 1.9 million inhabitants (as estimated in 2010); while its urban fabric extended rapidly 400 times approximately.

The rapid development of Dubai encountered with the challenge of the economic downturn in 2008. In response, Dubai Government took the opportunity to restructure its resources and economic trends. The need to review the spatial urban planning of the Emirate was emerged where some mega projects have to be deferred or put on hold, and the infrastructure networks required more consolidation.

Goals of the Initiative

Key to the Project was defining a preferred spatial direction and form that responds to the Emirate needs and growth to 2020, while enabling immediate possibilities for public and private investment to achieve sustainable growth to 2020 and beyond.

The Project seeks to optimize on existing government infrastructure investments; rationalize an integrated land use and mobility; protect key economic assets; and be flexible and responsive to the environmental challenges and constraints, and to the socio-economic transformations.

Innovation for the Initiative

The Project initiatives may be considered as evolutionary and revolutionary.

The innovations in Dubai follow the rules of 'changing challenge into opportunity'. In this Project, the innovation is applied in:

1. The strategic spatial planning approach for the whole of the Emirate, including defining the urbanization parameters within land and sea at metropolitan and regional levels.

2. Preparing the planning governance and legislative framework including promoting a 'Supreme Urban Planning Council'.

In spatial planning, the comprehensive context scan and analysis of the existing situation may be considered as borrowed method; but defining the urbanization parameters and the spatial structure planning constitute an inspired innovation that is unique to Dubai context.

In terms of planning governance, a comparative study with selective world cities were carried out related to the planning system adopted by each city. Dubai benefited from the study and recognized the need to set out a planning system that considers the major three components of managing spatial planning including:
    a. Strategic planning and plan-making.

    b. Statutory planning, and urban and environmental management.
    c. Development control and place-making.

Dubai considered such components and inspired a planning governance framework that is more responsive to Dubai specific governance requirements that complements the current planning system.

Obstacles and Solutions to the Innovation

The main obstacles may be summarized as follows:

1. The forecast of the growth of Dubai's hybrid population of which 90% are expatriates and their residency is mostly linked to their employment and to the challenging economic situation and growth.

2. The forecast of the economic growth and market conditions beyond 2008.

3. Dealing with the mega projects developments which were affected by the economic downturn after 2008.

4. Defining the desirable planning system that can best respond to Dubai's context.

The following trends were considered in overcoming the obstacles:

1. To overcome the socio-economic dimensions, the Project considered three scenarios; low growth, medium growth, and high growth. A consensus

achieved on medium growth with consideration towards high growth.

2. Staging and prioritizing mega projects were considered in conjunction with Dubai Government trends and the master developers in order to streamline development.

The Project promoted a new planning system that respects the current organizational structure of existing government departments, and the semi-governmental master developers companies. It considered 3 options that addressed the promotion of an efficient planning process and governance framework. The desirable option as adopted by the TEC was to establish an 'Urban Planning Supreme Council' (UPSC).

Outcomes and Assessments

Outcomes achieved are as follows:

Reflecting the vision for Dubai and the challenges and opportunities for sustainable and competitive urban transformation, a number of strategic actions were defined and incorporated into the Project hoping to achieve the following.

1. Protect and facilitate economic opportunities.

2. Define urbanization growth limits.

3. Consider flexibility for growth where required.

4. Consolidate the urban form and development projects by capitalizing on prevailing infrastructure and mobility, and conserve the natural systems.

5. Facilitate social needs especially housing and community facilities.

6. Broaden accessibility and mobility.

These issues reflect the anticipated desired broad outcomes of the Project at the Emirate scale-level.

Dubai already has a well established regional and global image. It is anticipated that further changes and outcomes will be perceived during this decade (up to 2020 horizons).

Since mid 2011, Dubai achieved successful international benchmarks related to social and economic dimensions.

Also, many Dubai government departments have taken advantage from the Project as a guide and commenced preparing strategic actions such as the property investment map, the education facilities map, the greening strategy, the sewerage and irrigation master-plan, review mobility infrastructure, energy diversification, etc.

Promoting the Project through international exhibitions and conferences, may also continue to contribute to the image of Dubai.

Chapter 23: Sustainable Urban Development in Dubai

Today, we live in a world where 'sustainable' urban development is no longer just a charitable 'greener' option but is the only sensible way forward. Many built environment professionals in Dubai realise that sustainability needs to be part of the grand plan of any society that is urbanising at the rate of that in many Middle Eastern countries, Dubai included and if regulation needs to be part of that thrust, so be it.

The limitless demand on energy and resources towards creating our urban built environment is fast catching up with the available non-renewable resources and in doing so, has brought irreparable damage to much of our environment. Working towards a sustainable urban growth, the building and regulatory authorities in most developed countries have integrated sustainable means and methods into building byelaws and statutory regulations. The urgency of making the trend global, and in particular in relation to in fast developing cities such as Dubai is the key point of this chapter.

Dubai Municipality's Zabeel Park, was opened in March 2006; the first of many. It offers play facilities, shade and greenery for a small entrance fee. New developments like Dubai Marina offer precious car-free public space.

Man's social well-being is intrinsically linked with his built and natural environment. The built environment more often than not has been governed by economic determinants, increasingly at the expense of environmental and ecological sustainability. Today, sustainability is perceived as a complex balance between economic, ecological and social factors, none of which should be prioritised at the expense of the other.

An important aspect of sustainable urban development is the 'ecological footprint' of developments or conurbations which implies the resources 'catchment area' that goes into the making or creating developments; an awareness most relevant to Dubai for reportedly topping the list. The 'One Planet Living' initiative popularised by the WWF towards self-containment and a sustainable environment has been a hallmark in the direction of sustainable development.

In the largely private building industry where financial feasibility continues to dominate extent of integration of sustainable methods in developments, the onus has been on building authorities to regulate, encourage and provide incentives for sustainable methods in conception, construction and operation of buildings. Authorities also need to be instrumental in spreading awareness about sustainable development and encourage its application in all urban systems including transportation, industries, construction and urban waste management.

One of the most important objectives for sustainable development is limiting CO_2 emission in the environment, a substantial waste product of urban systems including transportation, building construction and building operating systems. International initiatives like the Kyoto protocol have led countries to adopt policies (such as the European Directive and the UK Energy paper) towards using zero-to-low carbon energy sources and significant reduced carbon emissions.

Codes for sustainable buildings address energy efficiency, water efficiency, surface water management, site waste management and appropriate and efficient use of materials. Codes encourage 'Low Energy Design' which includes the following considerations.

1. Internal conditions – reduce internal energy loads efficient design, maximize day-lighting, passive.

2. HVAC, shading, insulation, solar control, thermal mass considerations.

3. Efficient environmental systems and services for heating, cooling and ventilation.

4. Commissioning and assessment.

Several countries have formulated their own Building Environmental Assessment Methods towards assessing and regulating sustainable urban developments. As yet, Dubai of the UAE has none.

Assessment methods need to be region-specific – depending on regional climate, available material resources, non-renewable and renewable energy sources, HVAC needs, construction methods, end users and operating costs.

It is often assumed that the cost of a sustainable 'green' building with its additional design input, specialised energy-saving systems, waste management and re-use systems and other operational requirements make it comparatively uneconomical when compared to the prevalent traditional building systems. The real picture unfolds on comparing 'whole life costs' of buildings taking into account their ecological footprint, energy and material consumption and waste management over the life of buildings. Research on 'whole life costs' has shown although the additional building cost of 'sustainable' buildings over the traditional ones are less than 2 per cent, saving on running costs are a significant 30-50 per cent and operating cost savings accrue to 5-10 per cent. The biggest and immeasurable savings is of the environment.

An integrated approach towards sustainable urban development addresses all stages in life of buildings, planning, design, construction and operation. It ensures immense benefits in quantity and quality of our built and surrounding natural environment. This 'sustainable' or 'lighter' living needs to become a global order for urban growth to be in harmony with the environment.

Chapter 24: Scaling Up Sustainable Urban Growth

In 2010, we quietly crossed a global threshold. The majority of the world went from living in rural areas to living in cities. As with foreign direct investment flows and the rise of atmospheric carbon-dioxide concentrations, this shift is a reminder that we live among imperceptible but significant megatrends.

By 2050, it is estimated that 70 percent of all people will live in cities, and the infrastructure needs to accommodate them and sustain this growth are massive, requiring a delicate balance of social, environmental, and economic considerations. As we have seen, urbanization can take multiple paths; sometimes resulting in cities that thrive, and other times creating cities with multiple tiers of poverty and disparity.

These trends make the case for sustainable urban growth appealing. We need to invest in sustainable infrastructure now because the lead times are long, the capital expenses high, and the systems that enable a lower per capital social and environmental footprint today will have exponential savings tomorrow. While the logic is sound, the growth of sustainable infrastructure has not kept pace with the need.

Over the past few weeks, I have had a chance to speak with several individuals in the private sector who are at the forefront of infrastructure development and who have shared their views on the challenges that business faces and what needs to change to make sustainable urban growth attainable.

Megacities: The future of urban growth

1. In 25 years, half of the world's population will live in emerging market cities.

2. Of the 25 fastest-growing major cities, seven are in China, six are in India, and none is in developed countries.

3. Per capital economic activity increases 10 percent with every 5-percentage-point increase in urban population.

4. By some estimates, cities are responsible for 80 percent of global carbon-dioxide emissions.

City focus

The conversation about opportunities to create sustainable cities has intensified over the past few years. One such effort, the CDP Cities project, allows cities to report carbon inventories in a similar model to the organization's widely used corporate climate disclosure platform. CDP Cities usefully built off the C40 Cities project, led by a group of like-minded city mayors with a long-term vision for energy reduction. Similar to the corporate-reporting platform, CDP Cities is a way to identify and manage risks and opportunities while creating the accountability to demonstrate improvements to a variety of stakeholders, including investors.

The global infrastructure and technology firm Siemens also entered the fray with its Green City Index, which ranks more than 120 global cities on a variety of environmental dimensions. Cities at the bottom have the greatest opportunities, and the ones at the top have the most lessons to offer (Detroit is dead last in the North America rankings and therefore has a significant opportunity for improvement and many lessons to learn). Siemens' index is also public, which helps catalyze a deeper discussion about the unique strengths and weaknesses of each region.

Cities are looking at sustainability as their strategy; we talk to cities about their strategy and goals just like we would with a company. City CSOs are making the same decisions as companies and have very similar challenges with internal engagement. How do one get the city departments like transportation, energy, utilities, and others out of their silos when they all have different needs? The best way is to sit down with city CSOs and learn about the struggles and challenges.

Just like in corporations, setting goals and having a vision proves to be an essential start for cities that want to engage business. The WBCSD Urban Infrastructure Initiative (UII) brings together 14 leading companies from sectors including energy, buildings, materials, transport, engineering, water, equipment, and support services to help urban authorities turn their sustainability vision into practical and cost-effective action plans.

One of the main success factors is the opportunity for direct and open dialogue. The companies in the UII are engaging collaboratively with cities upstream in the planning process, demonstrating the value of the early involvement of business and showing how a multi-sector group of leading companies can help cities find integrated solutions to interconnected challenges.

The UII project, which is working with nine cities around the world, has already produced three "solution landscape reports" for Turku in Finland, Tilburg in the Netherlands, and four cities in India's Gujarat state. The "solution landscape" presents a menu of potential options for cities to address their key sustainability challenges. One of the main success factors is the opportunity for direct and open dialogue. Business adds value by being involved in the beginning, looking at the big plan, and looking at the issues landscape and challenges. WBCSD decided to work with multiple companies as opposed to a more ad hoc engagement to encourage the idea that it was business, not just individual companies working with cities.

The WBCSD expects that companies will use the landscape reports to refine their own approaches to working with these cities, targeting specific challenges and opportunities.

Mismatched time frames

One significant challenge with deploying sustainable infrastructure solutions in cities is the vastly different time cycles used by business and government; because of these challenges, we recommends business engage on these issues early.

The time to intervene is now, before significant growth, and before there is a locked-down strategic plan. Our experience is that building trust is critical. There can be conversations about public-private partnership, and we can talk about what the private sector can bring to the table. The timing of this conversation is important.

Need for better coordination and understanding among governments, industries, and NGOs so that cities holistically plan for and build the infrastructure of tomorrow rather than create an infrastructure of mismatched components and potentially stranded assets.

Energy has a long development and life cycle, so buying the lowest-cost technology today doesn't usually create the infrastructure of tomorrow. Purchasing decisions need to take into account the full life cycle cost of technology, including operating and maintenance costs as well as potential disposal costs. This truly gives the technology of tomorrow fair weighting and consideration for its long-term value.

Aligning incentives and strategies

Like other transactional aspects of sustainability, most notably supply chain issues, getting the incentives right allows for greater transparency, better decision-making, and more "sustainable" sustainability solutions.

When we see cities stepping up and making policies and strategies in support of energy efficiency, that is a clear signal to us. City visions can vary dramatically, so it's important to understand their objectives. One of the cities we worked with in Europe, for example, was looking at all of the energy content in the city, while another in India felt its primary responsibility was to improve the efficiency of its public lighting. We cannot apply the same approach for both.

From 'smart cities' to 'wise cities'

We do a lot of analytics. When we crunch the numbers, cities get tired of hearing about 'smart.' Where is the wisdom? What is the outcome? Who are you today really? What kinds of problems are you having with poverty alleviation, for example? Who are you trying to become? What is the city you are trying to govern?

Much of megacity discussion ignores the fact that most of the growth will be in what are fourth-tier cities around the world (using China's commonly used but non-exact classification). This means that companies need to be more sophisticated in the Global South and emerging markets, and take time to understand the associated cultural components. For instance, understanding demographics is critical to creating solutions. The aging population is the fastest-growing cohort, yet most of our cities are designed by men for young men in commerce. How will women, children, and the elderly thrive in those cities?

How to fast-forward progress

City-focused initiatives, lead by NGOs and the private sector, are drawing more attention to the clear opportunities, but the results are still lagging behind the pace of the growing challenges. While innovation is important for developing sustainability solutions, technologies and infrastructure systems that will help achieve sustainable growth already exist.

Companies that provide infrastructure systems and components for energy, buildings, and transportation, must push fast-forward to deploy these technologies faster. They can start by collectively understanding the challenges and the role that each stakeholder sector can play in support of sustainable growth.

NGOs and civil society organizations can develop credible standards, decipher local issues, and create the environment that supports sustainable urban growth.

Government policies can create income distribution, economic and social mobility, the right incentives for the private sector to invest, space for truly engaged discussion, and a commitment to longer-term sustainability strategies.

Business can deploy systems that address real social and environmental challenges; along with the partnership of government and civil society rather than having to settle for incremental improvement and shorter-term sustainability gains.

We know that when business engages stakeholders proactively, the insights gained will lead to more informed decision-making, more valuable collaboration, and more inspired business models. The challenges are large, but the quiet and unstoppable megatrends are larger. The sooner meaningful engagement is at the forefront of the sustainable urban infrastructure agenda, the sooner we can hit fast-forward and have a chance at truly sustainable growth.

Chapter 25: Resilient Cities

By 2050, seven out of every 10 people on Earth will be an urban dweller. What the cities of the future look like depends largely on decisions we make today. Will we design a future where driverless cars zip around under sky-scraping vertical gardens in hyper-connected, energy-efficient "smart cities"? Or will we be trapped in endless traffic jams while pollution overwhelms remaining green spaces and infrastructure crumbles?

Nine billion people living well within the limits of the planet by mid-century. That is the simple but powerful "Vision 2050" that the World Business Council for Sustainable Development, or WBCSD, has for the future of humanity. There is no doubt that sustainable cities are central to this vision. Our cities can be the cornerstone of the green circular economy, supporting resilient societies and inclusive communities with universal access to public services and economic opportunity.

This future is absolutely possible; however, we must act now and take full advantage of the fact that much of our cities and infrastructure is not yet in existence, particularly in the developing world where urban growth is fastest. For example, more than 50 percent of the buildings to support the 300 million more city dwellers in China by 2030 are not yet built. We have a critical one-off window to create compact, mixed-use, transit-oriented urban centres incorporating sustainable, low-carbon infrastructure and prioritizing access and inclusion.

Central to realizing this opportunity is bringing together two of the most powerful forces we have for driving sustainability transformation; the leadership of city governments and the innovation and delivery capacity of the private sector. Building strategic engagement and "co-innovation" between cities and business has been the core focus of the WBCSD's Urban Infrastructure Initiative, or UII; 14 leading global companies and 10 cities around the world working collaboratively to identify innovative and practical solutions to help cities realize their long-term vision for prosperity and sustainability. The UII is one of a number of major local and global initiatives tackling the key challenges we face in driving a sustainable urban future. I know it is unfashionable these days to be an optimist, but I do believe that Vision 2050 can be a reality.

The complexities of contemporary global urban, political, economic and environmental issues are evident as we are confronted with the greatest challenge that we have faced. As we move toward 2050 we are facing the consequences of accelerating urbanization and population growth, the rise of mega-cities and mega-regions, the scarcity of natural resources and their mismanagement, the impact of major errors in our responses to disasters and the increasing demand for and complexity of greatly expanding transportation flows.

Our societies also have undergone rapid and radical shifts in terms of age and class, increasing inequities between the rich and poor and intense demands for democracy in the public realm. All of this requires immediate solutions but also change of worldviews from architects, urban planners, designers, landscape architects and urbanists. We need these professionals and experts to contribute their most imaginative, pragmatic, resilient, innovative and just solutions.

The way forward is sustainable and resilient cities; energy-efficient neighbourhoods and districts and green urbanism, but also civic design that will help shape and organize the city on basis of diversity, human scale and preservation. Equally important are the new visions for neighbourhood housing redevelopment that should support a human, economic, just, social and cultural recovery and renewal.

The systems and processes that we put in place to achieve these ends can be thought of as the software of the community, which includes formal societal services and institutions as well as the community's informal structure and cultural and social relationships. For any of this to happen, a major shift and change in habits, customs and adaptation to an uncertain future will be required from all citizens, and without a consensus of all, the vision of a 2050 sustainable and resilient urban world will not be possible.

By 2050 most nations on Earth will be highly urbanized, including Africa, parts of Asia and India, where presently only about one-third of the population lives in urban centres. In fact, between now and 2050 some of the largest cities in China and India will surpass Tokyo (currently with 35 million people) as the largest cities in the world.

Cities in 2050 will continue to perform their primary function as places of intense human interactions ("social reactors," as I like to call them), but in some ways will look and feel very different from what they look like today; especially those in the developing world. They will have to devise new ways to manage the congestion and the severe environmental impacts that beset them today. They will have to be safer, develop better governance and attract people from all over the world. Cities at their best are social environments where creativity and human development go hand in hand. The great challenge for cities in the decades to come is to promote universal socioeconomic development that is open-ended and sustainable.

This means achieving many age-old fundamental human aspirations, such as eliminating poverty and creating inclusive societies where equal opportunities are a reality and the "pursuit of happiness" is an attainable goal to everyone. To be sustainable, this also will mean that we will need new technologies to harness more energy, not less, and to generate it and use it in clean and safe ways, ultimately from fully renewable sources. This, together with improved "cradle-to-cradle" design, would allow us to recycle nearly all of what we consume, generating positive interactions between cities and Earth's natural environments.

Cities are dynamical environments capable of promoting great change very quickly. The universal attraction of cities today is a sign that this is becoming possible to everyone, especially in developing nations.

In the short term, however, urbanization and development are creating many of their familiar unintended consequences on a massive scale, including the growth of urban poverty, the severe inadequacy of older political structures, insecurity and massive pollution and greenhouse gas emissions, with potentially devastating consequences for climate change. Solutions to these problems are best found at the source in cities.

The greatest obstacle to successful urbanization is our present lack of the understanding of cities. As a consequence, much urban policy is often inadequate, short-sighted and unsustainable.

Through new communication and information technologies and citizen participation, it is now possible to create new types of urban infrastructure to share knowledge about very local conditions at the global scale. In this way, we may be able to cumulate information in a more interdisciplinary body of scientific knowledge about cities and use policy interventions as learning opportunities that transcend local conditions.

In China, urbanization is occurring at an unprecedented scale. By the end of 2012, the mainland of the People's Republic of China had a total urban population of 712 million or 52.6 percent of the total population, rising from 26 percent in 1990. It is projected that 70 percent of the population will live in urban areas by 2035. Over the next two decades China potentially will build 20,000 to 50,000 new skyscrapers and have more than 220 cities with populations of more than 1 million.

The romantic notion of future cities is that they will be smart, well-connected with zero-emission vehicles, powered by renewable resources and self-sustaining, and have buildings equipped with green technologies while still providing all the fun, excitement and ample economic opportunities for all residents.

Dystopian future scenarios also exist; where city residents and corporations fight over a resource-constrained world, cities are highly polluted and crime ridden, residents are monitored without any privacy, and there is a chasm of disparity between the have and have-nots.

We see glimpses of both futures in China now. There are cities with magnetic levitation trains able run at over 500 kph, super-capacitor public buses, electric cars and bicycles, smart traffic monitoring systems, LED Platinum-rated buildings and developments, smart personal devices and sensing technologies, record numbers of wind turbines and solar photovoltaic installations, and numerous eco/smart-cities planned. At the same time, cities in China are experiencing record pollution levels, unprecedented traffic gridlocks, loss of agricultural land and a high number of social protests over loss of resources.

The future of cities and their residents can be either bright or bleak or both at the same time. To chart the path, many questions will need to be answered. How will cities be powered? Can "waste" resources be used? Are buildings and infrastructure resilient enough for climate change? Where will our food come from? Are the needs of all residents being addressed? When does "censored" become censored? How will the lack of access to new knowledge and digital technology affect the poor and marginalized in terms of economic opportunities? Can we manage the use of resources in cities with the regenerative capacity of the ecosystem?

I think there will be both futures for cities. How we design, set policies, finance, govern and manage these immense challenges will define different futures for different cities.

I am optimistic that there is a great future for most of us in cities and that good design and policies eventually will prevail, but not until after we have learned plenty of tough lessons along the way. In order to see the best possible future for all, we have to ensure that everyone has a say rather than just a select few.

Contemporary cities have consisted of mostly single-purpose or single-use buildings. In the future I think we will see more and more vertical diverse buildings.

The Shanghai Tower in China is effectively a city within a building. You have multiple uses vertically that are stacked on top of each other. Going vertical is a really fascinating development and I expect we will see more of this.

The point where buildings become self-sustaining be it water and power neutral or water and power positive, meaning they give back more resources than they consume is certainly within the realm of possibility over the next three decades.

No matter where cities are situated, though, I think it's important that they are resilient to site-specific climate change issues.

I think the cities of tomorrow also need to consider the availability of open space and not only open space for a select group of people, but open space available to everyone. These spaces provide locations for idea exchange and a shared point of view where people can come together and see themselves as part of a collective community. The retention of open spaces will become increasingly important as land becomes more valuable in and around the centre of cities.

Effective urban planning for the future requires vision and will to create something with more vitality than what was there before; proposals with longevity and relevance for generations to come. If we use those as metrics by which we measure success for city building and planning, then we will be on the right course.

Chapter 26: Sustainability is Everyone's Responsibility

It's probably fair to say that historically, the live events industry was seen as throw away and wasteful. While this may have been the case, the industry has come a long way over the past few years. Sustainability is now everyone's responsibility, and venue teams have the potential to become market leaders in implementing effective processes to reduce their combined impact on the environment, setting a high standard for others to follow.

Venues can now introduce sophisticated and up-to-date lighting and heating technology into management programmes to reduce energy consumption. Waste streams across venues can be intensely analysed and identified, and with the introduction of a smart process in the segregation of waste streams, there's no reason why the majority of waste cannot be recycled, with no waste at all going to landfill. The NEC's Waste Pre-Treatment Centre is now part of day to day operations and integral to the sustainable success of the business.

At venues, additional features can play their part; shuttle buses now have economical Euro V engines and tracking software and drivers can be measured on their performance. Buses can also help push out a strong message for venues promoting use of public transport for the benefit of the environment. Water management systems in washrooms and the introduction of Smart Meters which can make us all more aware of the energy we use so we can take immediate action to reduce waste; are great examples of how small changes can have a great impact.

Education and support is a vital part of environmental performance, as is significant awareness and knowledge within venue teams. Engagement, in addition to working in partnership with stakeholders to provide assistance and advice, is also key to ensure buy in and to aim for the least possible impact on the environment from every event or exhibition. What we do today will affect the future of us all.

It's not a quick win, however. Venues need to be continuously looking to improve. Obtaining accreditation to ISO 14001 provides confidence in a team's ability to deliver its environmental policy, including the commitment to comply with legislation, prevent pollution, and to continually improve environmental performance.

The events industry continues to make great strides in its positive contribution to sustainability and a "greener" world, and sustainability is now part of day to day decision making. Venue teams have learned a lot along the way, and as an industry they will keep learning and developing good sustainability practices to ensure live events continue to be enjoyed in a healthy environment. We can't keep using earth's natural resources.

Chapter 27: Lessons from the Past and Ideas for the Future

Less than a decade ago, the companies investing in supply chain sustainability were primarily in the apparel, footwear, and toy sectors. Today, all industries prioritize supply chain sustainability, including the biggest brands in electronics, consumer goods, transportation, and other industries.

The number of standards has multiplied, reflecting a broader set of topics and participants. In the early 2000s, priorities were wages, working hours, and health and safety. Today, issues also include environmental performance and anti-corruption. Product certifications and labels have also exploded. An entire index exists just to catalogue the number of new eco-labels launched every year.

But what progress have we made toward improving the lives of workers in supply chains and protecting the ecosystems that support industry and commerce as well as human survival on this planet?

Although supply chain sustainability management practices have evolved significantly, we have an opportunity to re-examine traditional approaches and achieve measurable, dramatic improvements. Here, I suggest four lessons we can take from supply chain sustainability efforts to date, and four ideas we can apply to achieve greater impact going forward.

The road we have travelled

It's hard to capture all of the lessons learned during two decades of work on supply chain sustainability challenges, but four stand out as most important.

1. We must go well beyond monitoring. Social compliance monitoring was initiated to hold multinational companies accountable for maintaining good labour practices at supplier facilities. While this did illuminate working conditions and violations, it also spurred unintended consequences, including duplicative and burdensome audits, bribery and phony records, and a pass/fail mentality that drove problems underground. A retailer once told me that his company fired all the in-house social compliance staff in order to root out rampant bribe-taking, which suppliers had come to expect as a condition of doing business with that company. Third-party audit firms also faced challenges to combat bribery in their relationships with suppliers and brands and retailers.

Perhaps the biggest problem was that the monitoring approach failed to motivate suppliers to own the sustainability agenda. Among other problems, monitoring didn't revamp management systems to sustain compliance and encourage improvement over time.

The increasingly prescribed remedy to this is a "beyond monitoring" approach that includes management-systems assessments and supplier-development programs that address root causes, provide training, set milestones and incentives, and otherwise encourage suppliers to improve their management practices and performance.

2. We need a comprehensive approach to social, environmental, and ethical practices. The range of topics making their way into strategies, policies, assessment and improvement practices, and multi-stakeholder collaboration has broadened over time, and, happily, there are also a growing number of tools available to help.

Energy and greenhouse gas management is now a mainstream part of sustainable supply chain management, with the (World Business Council for Sustainable Development/World Resources Institute) WBCSD/WRI's Scope 3 emissions standard, the Carbon Disclosure Project's reporting requirements, and the Electronic Industry Citizenship Coalition's Carbon Reporting System representing just a few of the tools for companies to work with suppliers on energy issues.

Other supply chain environmental topics include air pollution, waste management, water usage and wastewater management, and impacts on land and biodiversity. Wal-Mart and Procter and Gamble have created supplier scorecards to collaboratively manage a range of environmental impact metrics (in addition to their labour standards programs). H&M, adidas, Nike, and others have committed to gradually phasing out hazardous chemicals, which follows Green Peace's high-profile detox campaign. Puma, which also committed to managing chemicals in 2011, released an environmental profit and loss statement that quantified and monetized supply chain impacts on greenhouse gas emissions, air pollution, water use, land use, and waste.

Over the past few years, due to new standards and legal requirements such as the UN Guiding Principles on Business and Human Rights and the U.K. Bribery Act, many companies have prioritized human rights and ethics. The concept of human rights due diligence and responsibility for managing impacts, no matter where they occur in supply chains, has also found its way into standards such as the OECD Guidelines for Multinational Enterprises (and OECD guidance on conflict minerals specifically), the ISO 26000 CSR Guideline, and the forthcoming update to the Global Reporting Initiative Guidelines.

3. It's important to look beyond the first tier of suppliers for the most significant impacts. The standards described above require companies to better understand their supply chains beyond the first tier.

The Guiding Principles, for example, require companies to "prevent or mitigate adverse human rights impacts that are directly linked to their operations, products, or services by their business relationships, even if they have not contributed to those impacts." In practice, this means that poor social and environmental management is now a concern both up and down the supply chain.

Specific industries have also launched efforts to move beyond the first tier of suppliers. In 2009, BSR's Mills

& Sundries Working Group started developing standards and tools covering labour, health and safety, and environmental impacts of textile mills and button, zipper, tag, and label suppliers. In 2011, the Sustainable Trade Initiative, a multi-stakeholder process funded by the Dutch government, launched a program in the electronics sector to focus on the second-tier suppliers in Southern China.

In addition, some of the most significant impacts from a lifecycle perspective often occur several tiers removed in the materials extraction and processing phases. In the realm of conflict minerals, Business for Social Responsibility (BSR) has discovered the imperative and challenges of working at multiple levels of the supply chain, from raw materials, to processing, to manufacturing, to retailing.

4. Integrating supply chain sustainability into core business practices remains the Holy Grail. The concept of "internal alignment" has become shorthand for ensuring that supply chain sustainability is built into core business strategy-setting and implementation across all departments and functions.

In BSR's Beyond Monitoring Working Group, they approached this on the practical level by sharing lessons across industries; for example, how to manage internal deadlines without causing overtime on the factory floor, and which information to review during supplier selection processes. They examined how e-learning and workshops can be used to educate and engage procurement staff, and they heard how companies were building supplier performance metrics into procurement staff evaluation and bonuses. Through our recently launched Centre for Sustainable Procurement, we are looking at how to integrate product and supplier sustainability considerations and information into procurement decisions.

The road ahead

We now know there is no silver-bullet solution to the complex and deep-rooted challenges in supply chain sustainability. So what does the future look like?

We encourage companies to focus on four things.

1. Set a vision for achieving positive impact. With both a business case and a moral case driving supply chain sustainability strategies, it is important for companies to evaluate (or re-evaluate) what they hope to achieve. Is it to do no harm? Increase market share of more sustainable products? Protect against business disruption while improving workers' livelihoods?

In our experience, companies typically travel through three main phases in their supply chain sustainability focus and objectives, and understanding where your company is currently might provide a useful frame for setting a vision.

a. Risk management: Identify, prevent, minimize, and mitigate risk of negative impacts on people, communities, and the environment. Companies pursuing risk management are usually trying to protect their reputation and minimize business disruption.

b. Supply chain improvement: Develop programs and practices to reduce negative impacts (labour standards violations, energy and water use, air pollution, waste) and increase positive impacts (improved worker well-being and development of healthy communities beyond the factory gates). Companies pursuing this approach are generally interested in achieving improvements in efficiency and productivity as well as maintaining and building their brand reputation.

c. Supply chain transformation: Make changes in products and production systems across the full value chain, from idea to execution. In addition to the benefits of the earlier phases, companies pursuing this approach are using supply chain management and engagement practices to support innovation and competitiveness.

Our vision is to see companies collaborate with their supply chains not just to solve problems but to make positive, systemic, and lasting change.

2. Focus on people, knowledge, and skills. "If only we knew then what we know now" is a familiar refrain. The past 20 years might look very different if we could send a time capsule to the past containing the wealth of experience we have gained. But we can take an important lesson forward. The world changes quickly, and our knowledge at any time is incomplete. We must improve how quickly we adapt our

practices, and build teams that have the necessary knowledge and capabilities.

3. Measure impact. In 2009, the Novo Nordisk Responsible Procurement group asked for help defining key performance indicators. To understand how other companies do this. They conducted an online survey and interviewed business leaders, investment analysts, and two NGOs that are active on supply chain labour standards. The results confirmed our hunch. Despite progress in measuring implementation at the customer and supplier levels, impact measurement is still in its infancy.

Impact measurement such as the work conducted by the Sustainability Consortium and the Sustainable Apparel Coalition helps identify areas for performance improvement and enables open, fact-based communications with stakeholders. We believe these efforts will help us achieve consistent and credible impact measurement for supply chains so that we can establish goals and accountability on the road to sustainability.

4. Get smarter about collaboration. Three priorities in collaboration deserve attention.

a. More comprehensive (and fewer) standards: If only we knew at the outset the problems that would be created by a proliferation of codes and practices for social compliance. Fortunately (and perhaps ironically), new platforms are emerging to enable convergence of these standards. For example, as a result of the European Commission's efforts, it's possible that in the next five years, we will have "stringent, prescriptive, and technically detailed lifecycle-based guidance" for conducting footprints of products across several environmental impact areas, not just greenhouse gas emissions. Standardization of social impact assessments in supply chains could be on the horizon as well.

b. More "professional" partnerships: In the past, partnerships were a murky area; today, there are clear and helpful practices for setting up and running collaborative efforts on supply chain sustainability, such as the ISEAL Alliance's codes for standard-setting, assurance (certification and accreditation), and impact assessment.

c. More portable data: The number and sophistication of information technology platforms that can link participants in supply chains has grown rapidly over the last few years. The Fair Factories Clearinghouse, Sedex, Eco Vadis, Achilles, and Aravo are just a few of the platforms and vendors for sharing information about sustainability performance in the supply chain. There is a real opportunity for technology providers to solve the data problem with easy-to-use, comprehensive, and standardized access to information technology that supports collaboration on supply chain sustainability.

What's Next

As we look forward, it's clear that the world will continue to look smaller and smaller, and that businesses will increasingly face natural resource constraints and social pressure to act responsibly. Businesses will be held accountable for impacts that may be several relationships removed from core operations, but still considered part of companies' supply chain sustainability footprints. With more standardized measurement and data visibility highlighting the many opportunities for improving sustainability impacts and more technology applied to solving problems; we will see solutions that we can't yet imagine today.

With these big ideas in mind, companies can consider some specific questions to help plan their own next steps.

1. What vision of supply chain sustainability aligns with your organization's goals and objectives?

2. Who are the internal champions who will dare to examine business as usual and identify areas for improvement?

3. Which external allies, from investors to academics to civil society organizations, will join you in addressing supply chain sustainability impacts?

4. What will your supply chain look like in 20 years, and what are the implications for your supply chain sustainability strategy today?

Chapter 28: Stakeholders Pressure

Stakeholder pressure from investors, shareholders, customers and nonprofits to push sustainability into the supply chain has significantly increased in recent years, with a record number of shareholder resolutions on supply chains issued. The recently launched Global Reporting Initiative (GRI) G4 Guidelines also requires an increased focus on sustainability throughout the supply chain.

By managing and improving environmental, social and economic performance throughout supply chains, companies can conserve resources, optimize processes, uncover product innovations, save costs, increase productivity and promote corporate values. Research shows the business case for supply chain sustainability is growing.

While more companies expand their sustainability programs to include suppliers, they struggle with implementation. The UN Global Compact's 2013 Global Corporate Sustainability Report finds that companies are increasingly talking about supply chain sustainability and making solid progress on setting expectations for suppliers. However, they are not yet supporting expectations with concrete actions that drive sustainability performance in their supply chain. Incidents such as the factory collapse and fires in Bangladesh highlight the need for increased and urgent actions in this area.

Incorporating sustainability into a company's supply chain is complex but the failure to act may be the biggest risk of all. Companies can take several initial steps to move toward sustainable supply chains.

1. Map your supply chain

Many companies do not have a comprehensive understanding of the sustainability impacts of their supply chain. An early step is to inventory suppliers, identify the most significant environmental and social challenges they have, and prioritize efforts with suppliers.

New Balance Athletic Shoe Inc. reduced the number of suppliers it does business with, in part based on performance against sustainability criteria. The company reduced its footwear supply chain by 65 percent and is focused on forming strong, positive partnerships with its suppliers. Some criteria that may be helpful for prioritizing suppliers include level of spending, importance to business continuity, and geography as a proxy for risk.

2. Communicate expectations

Focusing on sustainability within your supply chain is a great way to communicate corporate values and culture to your suppliers and customers. Establishing and communicating expectations through a supplier code of conduct is a critical step in involving suppliers in your sustainability efforts.

Many resources and tools have been created to assist companies with the development of a supplier code of conduct. For example, the United Nations Global Compact publication, "Supply Chain Sustainability. A Practical Guide for Continuous Improvement", has guidelines and tips for writing and adopting a successful supplier code of conduct. A new tool developed by the Global Environmental Management Initiative (GEMI) helps companies prioritize where in their organization's value chain they may have opportunities to improve supply chain sustainability, and then provides case studies of companies that have leveraged these opportunities.

3. Baseline supplier performance

Once you know who your target suppliers are and have set compliance standards, collecting data from suppliers through a simple benchmarking questionnaire or self-assessment will provide you an understanding of your starting point.

Many organizations, such as retailers, major brands and the U.S. Federal Government, have started evaluating the performance of their suppliers through questionnaires and surveys. Increasingly, organizations incorporate all areas included in their code of conduct with special focus and weight in the self-assessments related to areas that are important to their business. Our client work shows that more companies are aligning the content of their assessments with the GRI guidelines and CDP questionnaires. Some sectors, such as the electronics (Electronics Industry Citizenship Coalition Self-

Assessment Questionnaire) and pharmaceutical (Pharmaceutical Supply Chain Initiative Self-Assessment Questionnaire) industries, have developed industry-wide surveys to reduce the burden on suppliers of responding to multiple requests for information that varies in content and format.

The baseline assessments form the starting point for future programs to improve supply chain sustainability and help assess where the greatest need for improvement exists. For example, Pacific Gas and Electric (PG&E) uses response from the Electric Utility Industry Sustainable Supply Chain Alliance survey to gauge performance of its top tier suppliers on important aspects of environmental performance, including greenhouse gas emissions, energy and water usage, and waste generation. The information is used to compile the environmental metric in the annual scorecards for top tier suppliers and to identify opportunities to partner with suppliers to advance business practices in target areas.

Communicating back to suppliers in a constructive way is critical for future engagement and provides encouragement for improvement.

4. Develop training and capacity building programs

This is an important step in improving sustainability and driving behavioural changes throughout your supply chain. Many external resources are available to support these efforts and some are tailored to specific sector needs.

In our experience, one effective way to transfer knowledge across the supply chain is to leverage the best practices and case studies from top performing suppliers at annual vendor conferences, via online training modules and through capacity building campaigns. By showcasing the success stories of selected suppliers, companies not only recognize their efforts but also demonstrate the practical benefits of sustainability initiatives to others in the supply chain. For example, HP has established supplier and peer educator-run programs that have provided training to a large number of workers. Since the start of their capacity building program in 2006, HP has carried out 22 training programs in 12 countries on topics such as antidiscrimination, energy efficiency, labour rights and women's health. Through programs conducted jointly with its first-tier suppliers, HP has already trained 155 second-tier suppliers, leveraging the investment and knowledge-sharing efforts dedicated to Tier 1 supplier capacity building.

5. Drive performance improvement

Once supplier baseline performance is understood, an audit program can measure performance improvement over time. While in many cases, the self-assessments are completed by a corporate group, such as EHS, procurement or marketing, onsite audits can reveal local practices, behavioural challenges and practical opportunities for improvement that are difficult to identify through questionnaires alone.

Once your organization implements an audit program, be prepared to act on the findings by developing and executing corrective action plans by clearly communicating the results and your expectations to suppliers, developing a capacity-building program and, if necessary, terminating suppliers if non-compliance persists.

Assessments and audits paired with incentive programs that reward sustainability efforts have a greater ability to drive sustainability performance. Encouraging transparency and selecting or awarding more business to suppliers with stronger sustainability performance can be very effective in driving improvement. Where this is not possible, incentives greater access to your value chain, such as access to customers or clients also can be effective.

In an effort to avoid audit fatigue and to provide a common framework for evaluation, some industries have developed common auditing and assessment tools. For example, the Sustainable Apparel Coalition developed the Higg Index, a performance assessment tool for the apparel and footwear industries. The Electronic Industry Citizenship Coalition has developed the validated audit process that covers both social and environmental performance and includes an auditor certification program to drive for further consistency in audits. Chemical companies have formed a joint initiative called Together for Sustainability (TfS), with the mission of developing and implementing a global supplier engagement program that assesses and improves sustainability sourcing practices.

6. Join industry collaboration

Many companies recognize that complex supply chain challenges cannot be solved by individual efforts and that industry-wide collaboration is required. Working in a pre-competitive environment, peer companies that share similar supply chains can set common standards and best practices for sustainability performance and allow suppliers to be evaluated on the same metrics. These collaborations help prevent audit fatigue, training redundancy and mountains of paperwork for suppliers working to meet similar requirements from their customers. Working with your industry peers is a great way to share knowledge about the sustainability performance of your suppliers.

If you have a more mature supplier sustainability program, your company can do even more.

1. Develop and/or deploy robust tracking tools, including software solutions, to monitor supplier performance and improvement over time.

2. Perform a logistics assessment to determine where sustainability improvements can be made.

3. Integrate supply chain sustainability criteria into the procurement process.

4. Create a shift towards supply chain sustainability by leveraging your buying power and influence.

5. Expand your sustainability goals beyond your direct operations across your supply chain.

6. Encourage innovation.

But don't get caught by the biggest risk of all; not acting.

Good Luck!!

www.ingramcontent.com/pod-product-compliance
Lightning Source LLC
Chambersburg PA
CBHW071800200526
45167CB00017B/553